WRONG IS RIGHT AND RIGHT IS WRONG

DON LITTON

authorHOUSE®

AuthorHouse™
1663 Liberty Drive
Bloomington, IN 47403
www.authorhouse.com
Phone: 1 (800) 839-8640

Published by AuthorHouse 08/13/2019

The Holy Bible, King James Version, (KJV), New York: American Bible Society, 1999.
The Holy Bible, New American Standard Bible, (NASB), La Habra, CA:
Foundation Publications, for the Lockman Foundation, 1971.
The Holy Bible, New International Version, (NIV), Grand
Rapids: Zondervan Publishing House, 1984.
The Holy Bible, New Living Translation, (NLT), Tyndale House Foundation, 2015.
The Holy Bible, New Revised Standard Version Bible, (RSV), Division of Christian Education
of the National Council of the Churches of Christ in the United States of America, 1989.

ISBN: 978-1-7283-2212-4 (sc)
ISBN: 978-1-7283-2211-7 (e)

CONTENTS

ACKNOWLEDGMENT

Writing a book was harder than I thought and more rewarding than I could have ever imagined. No one in life does anything worthwhile alone. So, in my case I have several special people to acknowledge. My wife, Janice, has kept me comforted and has for years put up with my crazy schedule, mainly my daytime and nighttime hours being in reverse order. Her love for Christ and me has allowed me great freedom to execute my calling. The members of Friendship Baptist Church in Fishville, La "endured my preaching and teaching" for 13 yrs, until January of 2018. They were a captive audience for my stories and not so humorous jokes; they would even groan when I began to tell them.

I would not have made it this far in my book had not my sister, Rita Litton Ellis, spent countless hours reading, correcting, and revising sentences and paragraphs of my manuscript. More importantly, I thank God for the journey, age 73, and to have KNOWN HIM for 58 years. Being a reborn Christian, the Lord has guided me with HIS eye and it has been an insane walk with HIM. Only a foolish man would say I know a lot about God because in my case the more I have learned about HIM, the less I realized I know.

Note: This Book & E-Book, Wrong is Right and Right is Wrong is sponsored by one of my sons, Jared Richard Litton. May God Bless him, Guide and Lead him to the places that he should go and help him fulfill his spiritual assignment for his life on planet Earth.

INTRODUCTION

I truly believe the Word of God is living, staying relevant to each generation as we apply it to today. Indeed, it is sharper than any two-edged sword. So, when I came upon a verse such as **Isaiah 5:20**, it cuts through all the rhetoric, all the arguments, all the politics, all the religious talk and "Christian-ese" and gets to the heart of the issue.

> **"What sorrow for those who say that evil is good**
> **and good is evil, that dark is light and light is dark,**
> **that bitter is sweet and sweet is bitter"** (NLT).

This is a verse for such a time as this. For months, I and millions of others have been witness to this scripture being lived out in churches and on the national stage. It does not matter whether you are a Democrat or a Republican; this comes down to basic values and crosses party and denominational lines. I have seen what is Good called EVIL and what is EVIL called GOOD.

CHAPTER 1

WHY DOES IT HAVE TO BE WRONG OR RIGHT

In 1986, one of the songs high on the charts was entitled, "Why Does It Have To Be Wrong or Right" by Restless Heart. The words of the song explain that a couple was deciding whether or not to have an affair and questioned why it had to be black or white and why you had to hurt one to love another. The singer could not understand why there had to be any issue at all. That philosophy is a repackage of what was practiced 5 decades ago during the Sixties when some people followed the 'free love' and 'if it feels good, do it' reasoning.

That type of examining of morality and authority creates large gray areas and can be expected among the Lost or unbelieving. The disturbing thing is that this questioning has crossed over into the Church and we are seeing an open season on long-established doctrines, beliefs, and traditions. Indeed, I fear that the emerging church movement for all its talk of liberty is really a submerging into chaos and maybe a form of the error Peter discusses in:

II Peter 2:19 - "While they promise them liberty, they themselves are the servants of corruption: for of whom a man is overcome, of the same is he brought in bondage" (**KJV**).

II Peter 2:19 - "They promise freedom, but they themselves are slaves of sin and corruption. For you are a slave to whatever controls you" (**NIV**).

There are no nonessential doctrines or gray areas to God.

I have always said that if tradition is truth, treasure it and if tradition is just tradition then trash it, but I fear that many go to excess and are guilty of throwing the baby out with the bath water. I am not called a Maverick for nothing but there is nothing inherently wrong with organized religion since in Scripture we are given officers and told to do things in decency and order while maintaining sound doctrine and good works. It takes a bit of organization to do all that. It doesn't just happen. Have there been errors and even abuses? Certainly there have been such things, but just because people misuse a system or symbol or whatever does not make the thing in itself worthy of trashing. Redemption or restoration to its true form may be necessary but be very careful what you kick to the curb.

I have been deeply distressed for decades over the apathy of Christians when it comes to doctrines and associations. We seem to think that a profession of salvation is all we need to work and worship together no matter what doctrine is taught or who we associate with. In secular law, if John hangs out with Bill and Bill hangs out with a gang, John will be a suspect if Bill gets into trouble with the law. John may be innocent and may have just been in the wrong place at the wrong time, but because he and Bill spend time together, John will be brought in with Bill and most likely be suspected in the illegal activity. Because of this association, John's reputation will be ruined and he may lose friends and their respect. A man/woman is known by his/her friends...guilty by association.

I have found that it is tough enough to be perfectly sure of your friends who at least give verbal assent to the same doctrines and beliefs that you have. There are false brethren and folks that may learn the Christian language in order to befriend us. Some people who say they are Christians may in fact be genuinely confused about church doctrine or could be guilty of agnosticism, heresy and disbelief.

That is why we must always make our terms and beliefs perfectly clear and keep our associations tight but not so tight that we don't associate with anyone but those in our local church. Yet, we can't just throw open our arms and accept everyone that says they are of the brethren. An enthusiastic, accepting mindset can lead to destructive relationships and/ or a separation from our church brothers and sisters. Fact is, a trip to Guyana and a serving of poisoned Kool-Aid was the sad end for some misled believers. Doctrine is extremely important.

Matthew 5:17-20 - "17 Think not that I am come to destroy the law, or the prophets: I am not come to destroy, but to fulfill. 18 For verily I say unto you, Till heaven and earth pass, one jot or one tittle shall in no wise pass from the law, till all be fulfilled. 19 Whosoever therefore shall break one of these least commandments, and shall teach men so, he shall be called the least in the kingdom of heaven: but whosoever shall do and teach them, the same shall be called great in the kingdom of heaven. 20 For I say unto you, That except your righteousness shall exceed the righteousness of the scribes and Pharisees, ye shall in no case enter into the kingdom of heaven" (**KJV**).

Jesus fulfilled every jot and tittle of the law. There was no part that was nonessential to Him. It all mattered. **Verse 19 of Matthew 5** is a gauntlet slapped in the face of such thought and teaching. Break and teach others to break even the least commandment and you will be called least in the kingdom; whereas, if you keep them, you shall be called great. That sounds essential to me. Yes, we Christians are in the kingdom but our position is contingent on what we do with the least commandments as well as the greatest of commandments. Grace is not sloppy and our teachings should demonstrate the importance of every detail important to our Lord and Savior.

Matthew 23:23-24 - "Woe unto you, scribes and Pharisees, hypocrites! for ye pay tithe of mint and anise and cummin, and have omitted the weightier matters of the law, judgment, mercy, and faith: these ought ye to have done, and not to leave the other undone. Ye blind guides, which strain at a gnat, and swallow a camel" (**KJV**).

Some like to use this passage to decry all rules and standards as being hypocritical and legalistic. They talk about majoring on the major rather than majoring on the minor. It would appear they are right at first glance but what they forget is the part that while the Pharisees forgot the weightier matters they were right to tithe the mint and anise. He told them to do both. He didn't say worry about the essentials like law, judgment and mercy but don't worry about the non-essentials like tithing herb leaves. Nope, he said to do both. Both were essential. We may be attempting to emphasize what we think is major and ignore what is minor, errors that are very similar. There is not a gray area here. It is black and white, wrong and right.

To be able to call EVIL GOOD and GOOD EVIL it might be good to know which is which at the start but therein is the problem. Outside of a few key issues the Church at large wants to be open-minded, tolerant and gracious with doctrinal error and sin. They want to walk in semi-darkness or gray areas instead of seeking the full light. This passage clearly indicates that God is of the opposite opinion. He knows what is good and what is evil. He expects us to know as well. Black and white, wrong and right is not what our culture might desire but it is the will of God for us to tell them.

Hebrews 5:12-14 - "For when for the time ye ought to be teachers, ye have need that one teach you again which be the first principles of the oracles of God; and are become such as have need of milk, and not of strong meat. For every one that useth milk is unskilful in the word of righteousness: for he is a babe. But strong meat belongeth to them that are of full age, even those who by reason of use have their senses exercised to discern both good and evil" (**KJV**).

The problem is that even among Church leadership we seem to have a lot of well educated but immature Christians. They should be teachers by reason of their education or age in Christ but they have to go back to the first principles for remedial training. They are unskillful in the

Word because they have not exercised their senses. Therefore they cannot discern good from evil. Sadly, many have even forsaken the milk being content with a pacifier or a form of godliness. They have developed a taste for the fake and dislike the taste of fresh milk and have no teeth or stomach for a good Scriptural steak. Is it no wonder that they are sickly and shallow saints?

They have need to be taught again but who shall teach them since even the seminaries have forsaken meat and milk and instead offer up meals from imitation or rotted manuscripts? They in their own prudence and wisdom have tossed away God's Grade A Premium beef and substituted greasy fatty pork riddled with parasites making those that eat from their menu nauseous when someone tries to feed them the truth. That we are in an age of apostasy is no real surprise. They can't know right from wrong for they have foggy minds and cataract eyes from their poor diet and bad recipe books.

I King 3:9-12 - "Give therefore thy servant an understanding heart to judge thy people, that I may discern between good and bad: for who is able to judge this thy so great a people? And the speech pleased the Lord, that Solomon had asked this thing. And God said unto him, Because thou hast asked this thing, and hast not asked for thyself long life; neither hast asked riches for thyself, nor hast asked the life of thine enemies; but hast asked for thyself understanding to discern judgment; Behold, I have done according to thy words: lo, I have given thee a wise and an understanding heart; so that there was none like thee before thee, neither after thee shall any arise like unto thee" (**KJV**).

What delighted the Lord most about Solomon's prayer was that he wanted understanding to be able to discern good from bad that he might properly lead God's people. Can we who are leading God's flock be we Pastors or teachers dare ask for less? Isn't the warning that we teachers shall stand the stricter judgment incentive enough for us to make sure that we know good from evil? It is not only ourselves that we hurt by trying to play with gray areas or walk the tolerant tightrope. How many will we send to Hell or make ineffective because we do not speak with authority from the oracles of God? The Scribes and Pharisees had more questions than answers and twisted the truth to fit their desires. They liked tolerance and gray areas and are now in Hell.

Deuteronomy 5:32-33 - "Ye shall observe to do therefore as the LORD your God hath commanded you: ye shall not turn aside to the right hand or to the left. Ye shall walk in all the ways which the LORD your God hath commanded you, that ye may live, and that it may be well with you, and that ye may prolong your days in the land which ye shall possess" (**KJV**).

II Kings 22:1-2 - "Josiah was eight years old when he began to reign, and he reigned thirty and one years in Jerusalem. And his mother's name was Jedidah, the daughter of Adaiah of Boscath. And he did that which was right in the sight of the LORD, and walked in all the way of David his father, and turned not aside to the right hand or to the left" (**KJV**).

In the Old Testament we are commanded to not turn to the right or the left from any of the ways of God. There are no nonessential doctrines in that decree and no room for tolerance and gray areas. If that was expected of people that did not have the Holy Spirit indwelling them or had all the revelation of God, then how much more should we be seeking the exact and complete will of God in all things? While we cannot keep the law nor are required to do so for salvation would the Holy Spirit lead us into anything contrary to the will of God or His character? I think not!

James 1:16-17 - "Do not err, my beloved brethren. Every good gift and every perfect gift is from above, and cometh down from the Father of lights, with whom is no variableness, neither shadow of turning" (**KJV**).

James is telling us that God is not fickle or changeable. There is no variation with Him. His yea is yea and His nay is nay. There is no gray area with Him. The moon, for example, is all light on one side and all darkness on the other. It has no gray area. Whatever area that God has shed His light on has no shading or shadow. There is no darkness in Him and gray is a mixture of light and dark. Yea, we might be looking through a glass darkly but if we really want to know if an issue is light or darkness we can know. After all, we have His Word, His Spirit to lead us into all truth and the mind of Christ. What is our problem? Most of the time we don't really want to know. We become Pharisees and twist it the way we want or become Sadducees and just deny it completely.

God does not have two standards for His house. Paul said in **I Corinthians 11** that there was no such other custom for the Church on that topic. There was nothing to contend about. It is written, so let it be done. The theme or commands in the Epistles never changed for any of the Churches. What was meant for one was meant for all which is why Paul instructed the Colossians to read the epistle from Laodiceans. It helped them to spot the phony letters that were being circulated by comparing the ones they knew were from Paul. He didn't tell one group to eat blood and then prohibit someone else. One Lord, one faith, one baptism, one rule for all was the teaching given.

How many minds does Christ have? Why does one have liberty to do things and the other not? The way some teach it Christ is schizophrenic or has multiple personalities. **Romans 14 and 15** are often used to teach the concept of doubtful things so that one person can smoke tobacco if they have faith, but another person can't smoke tobacco because they have no faith. You can pick the issue in your neighborhood but it still comes down to a father telling his son to go out and get drunk but forbids his daughter to even drink one drink. It is an absurd teaching when you look at it in that context. That is the trouble we get into when we want to walk in gray and have no discernment between right and wrong or good and evil.

The problem is that those passages in **Romans 14 and 15** don't really teach that. He said not to spend time arguing about things but Paul told the pork eaters and those who ate meat used in the pagan temple that they were right to do so, provided the meat was sold in the marketplace. Don't do it. In the end, he says that the stronger brother was to give up his liberty in order not to offend and make the weaker brother stumble. You don't hear that preached much as that is one of the last things that American Christians want to hear. They will fight for their liberty unto death but will not die to self that they may be truly free!

Titus 1:9-11 - "Holding fast the faithful word as he hath been taught, that he may be able by sound doctrine both to exhort and to convince the gainsayers. For there are many unruly and vain talkers and deceivers, specially they of the circumcision: Whose mouths must be stopped, who subvert whole houses, teaching things which they ought not, for filthy lucre's sake" (**KJV**).

You must be able to discern good and evil if you are going to rightly divide the Word and to hold fast to it. When you know the Word it brings stability to your life and those around you. You must shy away from those that do not believe in sound doctrine. Why?

II Timothy 4:2-5 - "Preach the word; be instant in season, out of season; reprove, rebuke, exhort with all longsuffering and doctrine. For the time will come when they will not endure sound doctrine; but after their own lusts shall they heap to themselves teachers, having itching ears; And they shall turn away their ears from the truth, and shall be turned unto fables. But watch thou in all things, endure afflictions, do the work of an evangelist, make full proof of thy ministry" (**KJV**).

Titus 2:1 - "But speak thou the things which become sound doctrine" (**KJV**).

Welcome to the world of the 21st Century. There all sorts of Mars Hill dwellers out there and the Internet has made the hill virtual as well as topographical. People want to hear what they want to hear. You can believe anything you want because you can find a preacher or church that will teach it to your order. They aren't Burger King but <u>you can have it your way</u>! If you can't find one just start one and you will draw a crowd eventually and they will pay to feel good! But as we see in Titus we are under commandment to stick to sound doctrine not the popular doctrine. One successful fellow said that he would not preach doctrine. Well, the meaning of doctrine is teaching or instruction so in spite of what he says he is preaching doctrine though it appears that he doesn't know the meaning of the word. The question is what kind of doctrine is he teaching? Is it false or sound, wrong or right?

Why does it have to be wrong or right? Because God created the reality we live in and He has set natural and spiritual laws into place. We live better and longer when we are obedient to these laws then if we do not. He calls the shots. We are the created not the Creator. He has said that all His Word is important or essential and that we must be able to teach sound or healthy doctrine so that we can discern between good and evil, wrong and right so that we can lead His people and lead others to Him.

Maybe you are out there lost and deceived by false doctrine and muddling about in gray areas. Come to the Light of the World and allow Him to make your need of salvation manifest or clear as He puts the searching beam of His Word on your life revealing your sin and condition. He can take you out of darkness and bring you into the glorious kingdom of His light and love. Please let Him do so! My Brother and Sister, has your walk in grace been sloppy? Have you just ignored the Word on some issues because you thought them nonessential or just minor things?

Sometimes God tests your obedience and love in little things. One lady was seeking the filling of the Spirit and could not seem to get through to God. She had a rhinestone hairpin that she really liked. Once she felt that the Spirit was telling her to get rid of that hairpin. She thought it was a silly idea and ignored it. After all, it was just a little thing. She prayed and begged for a new sense of God's power in her life and to be filled but to no avail. One day as she was at her dressing table, the thought came to her once again to throw the hairpin away. This time she said, Lord if this is your will, so be it. When she threw it in the trashcan her prayer was answered. It was such a little thing, but it was enough to block her fellowship with the Lord for she had a lot of pride in how she looked when wearing the hairpin. After letting go of the object of that pride, the Holy Spirit could have complete control.

If you want God to Bless America Stop Legalizing Sin!

CHAPTER 2

CONFUSING EVIL WITH GOOD

Humanity has always been adept at confusing evil with good. That was Adam and Eve's problem, and it is our problem today. If evil were not made to appear good, there would be no such thing as temptation. It is in their close similarity that the danger lies. Modern social righteousness often differs from the righteousness of the Bible. Someone has said: "A wrong deed is right if the majority of people declare it not to be wrong." By this principle we can see our standards shifting from year to year according to the popular vote! Divorce was once frowned upon by society, and laws against fornication and adultery were strictly enforced. But now divorce is accepted by society, and fornication is glorified in our literature and films (Graham, 2018).

The Bible says: **"Woe to those who call evil good, and good evil."** His standards have not been lowered. God still calls immorality a sin, and the Bible says God is going to judge it.

God has not changed!

Honesty was once the hallmark of character. But it has been set aside with an "It's all right if you don't get caught" philosophy. It seems that only when we are in court are we required to tell the truth, the whole truth and nothing but the truth.

Evil worms its way into our lives by presenting a harmless appearance, such as the full-page, full-color ads of "the man of distinction," dressed impeccably, sipping a glass of whiskey with his friends in the warmth of a well-appointed room. Such ads say nothing of the new alcoholics that are being made every day, nor of the problem of excessive drinking that is eating at the heart of our civilization. It wouldn't be in good taste, but it would be honest. **"Woe to those who call evil good!"** The young couple, though they have been warned of the psychological and spiritual dangers of premarital intimacies, sit in a parked car and flirt with tragedy, all the while calling the experience heavenly. That which is heavenly within the marriage bond can become a hell of remorse to those who indulge in it outside of marriage. **"Woe to those who call evil good!"**

How do we get our values so mixed up? How do we fall into this trap of Satan? For one thing, we're shortsighted. We look for shortcuts to happiness. Our lust for immediate pleasure prompts us to think of evil as good. In one of novelist John Steinbeck's books he has a character saying: "If it succeeds, they will be thought not crooked but clever." In our desire to achieve success quickly, it is easy to get our values mixed up and call evil good and good evil.

- Another way to call evil good is to say that morals are relative.

Someone has said: *"As the occasion,* so the behavior." We have changed our moral code to fit our behavior instead of changing our behavior to harmonize with our moral code. Nothing is firm today. We are not on solid ground. Young people are shifting from one side to the other. Morally, they are drifting aimlessly without compass or guide.

- Still another way that evil is called good is for the conscience to be perverted.

And certainly our consciences today are perverted. But right is right even if nobody is right, and wrong is wrong even if everybody is wrong. God does not change the moral law to suit our behavior.

We accept in stride the false promises of politicians, the misrepresentations in advertising, the everyday dishonesties of Mr. and Mrs. John Doe, the cheating on exams, the usual exaggerations in conversation and the common immoralities of our times. We no longer blush, and we're no longer shocked by the immorality that's going on around about us. **"Woe to those who call evil good!"** The modern conscience has been twisted and distorted so badly that it is difficult to tell what is genuine and what is false.

- *Self-centeredness* is another reason we are so inclined to call evil good.

When something brings profit or pleasure to us we are inclined to call evil good, even though we know it is dead wrong. *"But it's what I've always wanted,"* or, *"It's good for me, although I know it's wrong"* are the alibis we have manufactured to justify evil and call it good. If we could only focus our eyes outward instead of inward and heed the words of Jesus:

Matthew 6:33 - "But seek first the kingdom of God and His righteousness, and all these things shall be added to you" (**NIV**).

Our trouble is that we say about Christianity what we say about everything else: *"What's in it for me?"* In our selfishness, we think of God as we think of everyone else in terms of what He can contribute to us personally. In other words, we want God to be our servant. **"Woe to those who call evil good!"**

- Also, through a popular technique called *Rationalization.*

We find it easy to call evil good. How easy it is to place the blame on others, on circumstances or on fate. From Adam, who said: "The woman whom You gave to be with me, she gave me of the tree, and I ate," to a member of the Senate who says: "I did nothing that a thousand other men would not have done," we excuse ourselves. We call evil good.

Our Lord was impatient with our tendency to rationalize our evil and call it good. In **Luke 18**, He told of the self-righteous Pharisee who stood and prayed: "God, I thank You that I am not like other men—extortioners, unjust, adulterers, or even as this tax collector" (**verse 11**). The Pharisee kidded himself into thinking he was something when he was not. He was skilled in the ancient and modern art of rationalization. But the tax collector, whom the Pharisee looked upon as the most sinful of men, saw himself as he was, and said: "God, be merciful to me a sinner" (**verse 13**). Jesus said: "I tell you, this man went down to his house justified rather than the other; for everyone who exalts himself will be humbled, and he who humbles himself will be exalted" (**verse 14**).

How can we get our values straightened out? How can our warped judgment be brought into line? How can we stop calling evil good? Some tell us that *Education* is the answer to these questions. Prove to people that crime doesn't pay, that illicit sex is psychologically harmful, that excessive drinking is harmful to the body and brain, that honesty is the best policy. "Let knowledge redeem them," they say. Others say that *Science* is the answer. Science can make a clean bomb. Science can make a harmless cigarette. Science can cope with the problems of alcohol. Science, they say, can tap the brain of man and alter his desires and make him civilized. Science, some proclaim, is the answer to the problems of man (Graham, 2018).

But the *Bible*, which has withstood the ravages of time, tells us a different story. It says that we possess a nature that wars against us, that seeks to destroy us. The Apostle Paul said:

Romans 7:21 - "I find then a law, that, when I would do good, evil is present with me" (**KJV**).

Evil is present in us disguising itself as good, controlling us and deceiving us. Sin is why the atonement was necessary. Christ died on the cross to make us one with Him, dead to sin and alive to righteousness.

Man without God is a contradiction, a paradox, a monstrosity.
He sees evil as good and good as evil.

That is why some people love evil and hate that which is good; they are still in their sins. For them, life's values are confused. Paul found the cure for his violent, destructive disposition, not at the feet of Gamaliel or in the culture of Greece, but on the Damascus Road when he met Jesus Christ. Later he wrote:

Romans 8:2 - "Because through Christ Jesus the law of the Spirit who gives life has set you free from the law of sin and death" (**NIV**).

Before his conversion, he saw Christ as the greatest evil and breathed out "threats and murder against the disciples of the Lord" (**Acts 9:1, NIV**). But after he encountered Christ on the Damascus Road, he loved what he had so fervently hated. At last he could see evil as evil and good as good, and, according to:

Acts 9:18 - "Immediately, something like scales fell from Saul's eyes, and he could see again. He got up and was baptized" (**NIV**).

His values were straightened out because his nature had been changed by the redeeming grace of God. Christ can do the same for you. When Paul heard the voice, he said:

Acts 9:6 - "Now get up and go into the city, and you will be told what you must do" (**NIV**).

15

Jesus Christ is calling you out of a world of delusion and deception in which evil is called good and good is called evil. Only if the scales fall from your eyes can you acknowledge Him as Lord.

You must have a personal encounter with Jesus Christ.

CHAPTER 3

CALLING EVIL GOOD

I want to look at a story that I think is familiar to all of us. It takes us way back to the beginning. And from this we'll see that the big issues we face today are not new, but they have been around since the beginning of time. And, indeed, they have been plaguing humanity from the beginning of time. In God's creation of the world, we see the statements in **Genesis 1** that God saw that it was "good" (**Genesis 1:4,10,12,18,21,25**). Then in **verse 31**, he says that it was "very good" or "excellent." Here, God is making a statement about creation. He is saying that his creation is good. Now, **GOOD** we know describes an ethical or a moral quality. *It describes value.* It also describes the lack or opposite of evil (Graham, 2012).

While the fact that God called creation good is of itself significant, I want to draw attention not to the goodness itself, but to the fact that it was God who was making this judgment. It was God who decided that the creation was good.

Genesis 2:16-17 says, "And the LORD God commanded the man, "You are free to eat from any tree in the garden; but you must not eat from the tree of the knowledge of good and evil, for when you eat of it you will surely die" (**NIV**).

God introduced the first rule to mankind. And here we may say many things, but again this is not my focus. Just notice, based on the fact that they are going to die if they eat from this tree, that this tree *Is Not Good* for them. Whatever we can say about this tree, it is not good for food.

Now we go to chapter three, the moment of crisis. The serpent came to tempt Eve into eating the fruit, and then give some to Adam. There are a lot of elements we could look at here, but I only want to look at Eve's statement for now. She had the command of God not to eat the fruit. She knew because she told the serpent about it. She had the *Word from God* telling her that this fruit was not good for her, because it would cause death. But in:

Genesis 3:6, we see Eve's response to the serpent's temptation, "When the woman saw that the fruit of the tree was good for food and pleasing to the eye, and also desirable for wisdom, she took some and she ate it" (**NIV**).

Up until this point, only God had made judgments about whether something was good or not good. God said that creation was good or very good. In **Genesis 2:18**, it was God who said that it was not good for man to be alone. And in:

Genesis 2:16-17 - "And the LORD God commanded the man, "You are free to eat from any tree in the garden; but you must not eat from the tree of the knowledge of good and evil, for when you eat from it you will certainly die" (**NIV**).

When giving the command about the tree, God calls it the tree of the knowledge of good and evil. Again, the word used here is the simple word for good and the simple word for evil.

Mankind did not have any need to know good and evil, because this sort of judgment is not his place. Indeed, sometimes I've struggled with trying to understand what is so bad about knowing the difference between good and evil. How can we avoid evil if we don't know what it is? How can we do good if we don't know what it is? Surely, it is not that God wants us to be ignorant. But what this tree did, was cause mankind to forget God's assessment of what is good and what is evil, and try to make his own assessment.

It takes mankind from hearing the voice of God and obeying it, to looking around and making a determination for himself. Eve made the first assessment of something's value, not only apart from the Word of God, but contrary to the Word of God. She assessed, by looking, that the tree was "good" for food. But she was deadly wrong. Eating from that tree was the worst thing she could ever have done for herself. It led directly to the judgment of God that follows later in the passage. And as we know, it led to the curse of death that still 6,000 or so years later, plagues the earth.

As if to make sure that we don't overlook this point, Eve is not the only one in the beginning of Genesis that makes this mistake. Go with me please to:

Genesis 6:1-3 - "When human beings began to increase in number on the earth and daughters were born to them, the sons of God saw that the daughters of humans were beautiful, and they married any of them they chose. Then the LORD said, "My Spirit will not contend with humans forever, for they are mortal; their days will be a hundred and twenty years" (**NIV**).

Here in the English, we have the translation that the daughters of men were "beautiful." Now, this passage is one of the frequently argued passages in the Old Testament. Who were the sons of God? Who were the daughters of men? What was the sin? But at least for now, we can overlook some of these questions and get right to the heart of the matter.

What did these "sons of God" do that was so bad? Once again they made a judgment. They made a judgment about whether something was "good" or not good. And once again, they made this judgment based upon their sight, instead of based upon the Word of God.

Mark 10:18 - "Why do you call me good?" Jesus answered. "No one is good except God alone" (**NIV**).

And even **Genesis 6:5**, "The LORD saw how great man's wickedness on the earth had become, and that every inclination of the thoughts of his heart was only evil all the time" (**NIV**).

God's assessment of mankind is "no one is good" and that man is only evil all the time. But the sons of God in this passage were not interested in God's assessment. Maybe they had the Word of God like Eve did and maybe they didn't have the specific Word of God yet, but the fact is that the assessment they made based on their own sight was wrong. Here, even after consuming the fruit of the knowledge of good and evil, mankind is no more capable of telling the difference between good and evil than he ever was. He is just as much a desperate failure as before and the reason for this is simple. *The assessment of goodness is left to God and God alone.* For only God is able to accurately make that judgment. When we try to assess things ourselves, we end up mixing up the values. Therefore we have this scripture in the Word of God (Graham, 2012).

Isaiah addressed this issue in **5:20**, "Woe to those who call evil good and good evil, who put darkness for light and light for darkness, who put bitter for sweet and sweet for bitter" (**NIV**).

Our society has had a tendency to do this for many years and now I fear that it's beginning to creep into the church. Our society says that what is right and wrong is up to you. What is good for you may not necessarily be good for me. And what is bad for you, might not necessarily be bad for me. But this is a lie. This is the same lie that caused Eve to eat the forbidden fruit. This is the same lie that brought the judgment of

God on the sons of God in **Genesis 6**. This is the same lie that brought judgment on Israel in the days of Isaiah. And this is the same lie that will bring judgment upon us if we buy into it.

Now, I don't know many Christians who would make the same statements as the world that morality is relative. But we must be careful that while we're fighting against moral relativism on the front side, that it's not creeping in through the back door. You see, just like Eve had the Word of God, which told her that the tree was not good for her, we also have the Word of God. We have the Bible, the Word of God, which clearly tells us what is good and what is evil. God, knowing that were incapable of properly assessing goodness, laid it out for us.

The Bible lays out the way that we should live. It lays out the types of things we should do and shouldn't do. But it seems that sometimes we want to refer to the Bible as just a guidebook. When we have a decision to make, we use the Bible as a reference point to try to make a good decision. We use the Bible as a reference point, from which we decide what is best for us. But his goes against the very nature of the Bible. The very reason for God giving us his Word is that he knows that our judgment is faulty. He knows that if the judging is left up to us, we will make the wrong choice every time. He knows that we will end up calling good evil and evil good. So he has laid out the answers for us. He has told us what is good and what is evil, so we don't have to rely on our own faulty judgment.

The first word of **Isaiah 5:20** packs a lot of meaning. It's a simple word, **"Woe"** and yet it says so much. It's important to listen to God's Word, which will allow us to recognize good vs. evil. It is so important that Isaiah says "woe" to those who don't listen. Woe to those who make this wrong judgment. And what is this word "woe." This word describes more than just coincidental misfortune. This woe will occur for those who confuse good with evil. It's not just harmful and it's not only natural consequences that will be endured.

When we do harmful things, there are often natural consequences. But when "woe to those who..." is used in the Old Testament it means one thing. It means the judgment of God is coming. It is an introduction to the judgment of God. The woe that comes to the one who makes a wrong judgment about good and evil is nothing less than the direct judgment and fury of God. When we refuse to hearken to the Word of God, and insist upon making our own judgments of what is right and wrong, then we are inviting the wrath of God into our lives.

The Bible is not a book full of suggestions. Some individuals determine the validity of the Bible based on our own personal experiences. But in practice don't we often do the same thing. We read the Bible as if it's supposed to give us some suggestions. And if we read something and we think, "oh that seems like a good idea" then we do it. But when we read something that we don't think will be beneficial to us we just ignore it. Or maybe we question it. We start to wonder why we have to do this thing. Or why we can't do this thing. And until we get our answer, we don't do it (Graham, 2012).

The Bible is not simply a guideline. We don't have to understand the reason behind God's commands to obey them. We don't have to know why something is good or something is evil in order to obey it. In fact, that's the whole reason that God gives us commands. He knows that we are unable to properly differentiate between good and evil. I think it's okay to ask God questions. It's okay to try to understand things. But we cross the line when we refuse to adhere to God's word until we completely understand it. Do you think Eve knew why she wasn't allowed to eat from the forbidden tree? She only knew one thing about that tree. God said not to eat of it or she would die. And that should have been enough information for her to run as far away from that tree as she could. That should have been enough, that God said it was not good for her, to keep her away. But it was her distrust of God and His Word that led her to eat of that forbidden tree.

This brings us back to the Garden of Eden, and back to what is the biggest element of obeying God's standards of good and evil, whether we understand them or not. That element is faith or trust.

Romans 10:17 says, "Consequently, faith comes from hearing the message, and the message is heard through the word of Christ" (**NIV**).

Faith comes from one thing, and that is hearing the Word of God. Eve heard the Word of God. She had the Word from God that said, "Do not eat of this tree." She heard his voice. But she also heard another voice. And that was the voice of the serpent. And in the beginning of **chapter 3**, the serpent begins to make Eve doubt the Word of God.

He begins to make her doubt even the very character of God. Instead of God making this judgment of good and evil for her, now she perceives it as God manipulating her for his own benefit. She listened to the voice of the "craftiest of all the creatures" instead of listening to the voice of the God who had lovingly created her. She allowed herself to doubt God's words. See for her, it was no longer a decision of did God say it or not. She knew he did. It wasn't even a choice of would she obey God or not, at least not in her mind. It wasn't even a question of whether God knew what was best for her. She went even deeper to question whether God even wanted what was best for her. In God's judgment of Adam, we see that he is guilty of the same thing.

Genesis 3:17a - "To Adam he said, 'Because you listened to your wife and ate from the tree about which I commanded you...'" (**NIV**).

Was it a sin for Adam to listen to his wife? No. If she had said, "Don't eat from this tree," then of course he should have listened to her. The emphasis here is that Adam listened to the voice of his wife, instead of listening to the voice of God. This was the tree "about which I commanded you." Adam had received the Word of God. Even though we don't know just how he jumped from trusting in God's Word to trusting in Eve's words, we know that he got there. Adam, like Eve, chose to listen to a voice who did not know, instead of the One Voice who knew all.

And we have voices all around us. We have people who whisper all kinds of Satan's ideas in our ears. Our very society is so turned against God that just in living here we are bombarded with messages that are contrary to God's Word. I don't want to get into too many specific examples, because I could go on indefinitely. But when our children go to school, they're taught that God didn't create the world, but it just happened by chance. They're taught that being gay is perfectly normal. Through "safe sex" messages they are taught that it's acceptable, perhaps expected, to be sexually active before marriage. These teachings go against teachings of the Word of God, so choices have to be made.

I'll tell you, when I was in high school, I didn't have all the answers to refute evolution. I know a lot more now than I did then, but at that time, I knew very little that would help me. It came down to a choice. It was a choice of whether I would believe my science teacher or my God. Even when it seemed like what my science teacher said made perfect sense, I had to choose to believe my God, who sometimes it seemed made no sense at all.

The Bible has a message of morality that we in the Church have done a good job of preserving, at least in theory. But the fact is, that the Bible has a very strong ethical message too. God is very concerned about how we treat other people. God is very concerned when we take advantage of someone, gaining at their expense. But what does the voice of our society say? The voice of our society says, "That's the way business is done." Everybody does it. We're just trying to feed our families. We're willing to overlook something that we know God's Word says is wrong, because it doesn't seem to work in real life.

We hear voices about faithfulness to spouses and families, how to raise kids, how to be successful, and a host of other things. And more often than not, the messages we hear conflict with what the Bible says. The trouble is that many times these messages make sense to us. Many times, we hear voices that sound like friendly voices. But these voices have only one aim. Their only goal is like the serpent in the Garden, to discredit the Voice and the Word of God. Trusting in God is listening to the Word of God, and obeying the Word of God, even when all around us we hear messages that it isn't true.

Another mistake that Eve made is the reason that I think we are so often willing to listen to these other voices instead of the Voice of God. You see, Eve didn't just hear the voice of the serpent and decide that the fruit was good. She didn't reason in her mind and conclude that the fruit was good. And she certainly didn't believe that the fruit was good. But as **verse 6** says, she **SAW** that the fruit was good. Eve looked at the fruit. And the fruit looked good to her eyes. Again, in the passage we were looking at in **Genesis 6**, the sons of God "saw" that the daughters of men were good. Here we have a contrast again. The Word of God says the fruit is not good. But now not only does the voice say that the fruit is good, but the sight says that the fruit is good. Naturally, if God didn't want us to look at the things, he wouldn't have given us eyes. Indeed, if he didn't want us to appreciate beauty, he wouldn't have made creation so beautiful. But here the sight I think refers to the senses or the physical senses. That is to say that the "unseen" is the spiritual. Faith is a spiritual thing (Graham, 2012).

But we, like Eve, have a choice. Will we be believe and trust in the God and His Word that we cannot see, or will we trust in what our senses tell us. You see, the purpose of the voices is to get us to look. The voices that contradict God's Voice get us to look at our circumstances. They may get us to look at our circumstances and evaluate God's Word in light of our circumstances. So, we may look at something the Bible says and think that it's a good suggestion and may even be possible in an ideal world, but it just doesn't work in your real world.

But the simple message that I come with today is that the Word of God does work. If we haven't seen evidence of that, maybe it's because we are leaving out significant portions. Let me give you an example. What if I teach you how to fish. First you tie the hook. Then you put the worm on the line. Then you throw the line in the water. Then when you feel a tug, you jerk the line. Then you reel in the line. Then you enjoy your fish for dinner. And you read my list, and say, "Well these are nice suggestions, but I really don't want to kill a poor worm." So you just skip that one step. Well, you're not going to catch any fish. Or if you don't know how to tie a knot, so you just sort of hang the hook on the end of the string, you're going to lose the hook and you're not going to catch any fish. Or if you get a bite, but you say, "You know I really don't think I should reel this in." You're not going to get a fish (Graham, 2012).

In order for this plan to work, you have to follow all the steps. The Word of God is like that. It works. It really does. It's not just some theoretical theology. It's not just something for us to study, so we can feel smart. It works. But, we have to do it. If we don't obey God, it won't work. If we start to second-guess God and decide which parts we'll obey and which parts just aren't for us, it won't work. If we start to listen to voices around us that tell us which parts we can't really be expected to do. If we start to look at the circumstances of our life and determining which parts of God's Word will fit and which won't, then it's not going to work.

The life lived in light of the Scripture is the life that works. But the life lived in light of God's Word is first and foremost, a life of faith. Before you can approach any of the individual mandates of Scripture in a meaningful way, you must first take the leap of faith, to trust the God of the Word. You must place your life in His hands, knowing that He knows better than you what is good and evil. And when you ignore the voices and the sights around you, you won't mix up good and evil, for God has already laid it out for you. The life of trust doesn't allow for selective obedience. It's all or nothing. Let's give ourselves to following ALL of God's Word. And then we will see that we will inherit ALL of God's promises.

The Word of God really does work!

CHAPTER 4

WHY DO THEY CALL GOOD EVIL AND EVIL GOOD?

E vil worms its way into our lives by presenting a harmless appearance, such as the full-page, full-color ads of "the man of distinction," dressed impeccably, sipping a glass of whiskey with his friends in the warmth of a well-appointed room. Such ads say nothing of the new alcoholics that are being made every day, nor of the problem of excessive drinking that is eating at the heart of our civilization. Of course it wouldn't be in good taste to show a picture of a "man of distinction" on Skid Row who began his drinking on Fifth Avenue but is ending it in the Bowery. It wouldn't be in good taste, but it would be honest (Forrester, 2016).

Romans 8:6-7 - "For to be carnally minded is death; but to be spiritually minded is life and peace. Because the carnal mind is enmity against God: for it is not subject to the law of God, neither indeed can be" (**KJV**).

If we do not seek God, we will be depending on our own carnal mind, which is "enmity against God" and at war with God. Evil men will not seek God.

Psalm 10:4 says, "The wicked, through the pride of his countenance, will not seek after God: God is not in all his thoughts" (**KJV**).

Evil men call good evil and evil good because they are not seeking God and are depending instead on their own carnal mind. Depending on your own will instead of on God's will is a type of rebellion (Forrester, 2016).

Luke 16:13 says, "No servant can serve two masters: for either he will hate the one, and love the other; or else he will hold to the one, and despise the other. Ye cannot serve God and mammon" (**KJV**).

Mammon is money and the love of money is the root of all evil.

I Timothy 6:10 - "For the love of money is the root of all evil: which while some coveted after, they have erred from the faith, and pierced themselves through with many sorrows" (**KJV**).

If we do our own will we are not serving God, but we are serving ourselves. We can't do both. If you serve yourself (and thus love the world) you cannot love God or be filled with God's love

I John 2:15-17 - "Love not the world, neither the things that are in the world. If any man love the world, the love of the Father is not in him. For all that is in the world, the lust of the flesh, and the lust of the eyes, and the pride of life, is not of the Father, but is of the world. And the world passeth away, and the lust thereof: but he that doeth the will of God abideth forever" (**KJV**).

In **Mark 9**, Jesus Christ said to remove what causes you to sin (or be offended) lest you be cast into Hell.

Mark 9:47-48 - "And if thine eye offend thee, pluck it out: it is better for thee to enter into the kingdom of God with one eye, than having two eyes to be cast into hell fire: Where their worm dieth not, and the fire is not quenched" (**KJV**).

Sin can lead to spiritual separation in Hell (death).

Romans 6:16 says, "Know ye not, that to whom ye yield yourselves servants to obey, his servants ye are to whom ye obey; whether of sin unto death, or of obedience unto righteousness" (**KJV**)?

We need to deny ourselves, take up our cross, and follow Jesus. Jesus Christ told us to do this in:

Mark 8:34-35 - "And he called to him the multitude with his disciples, and said to them, "If any man would come after me, let him deny himself and take up his cross and follow me. For whoever would save his life will lose it; and whoever loses his life for my sake and the gospel's will save it" (**RSV**).

Verse 35 tells us that we need to lose our lives, our pursuits, goals, and fleshly desires which are apart from God's will. If we chose our own will over God's will, God is then not the one we are serving. We would be serving ourselves instead of God. Remember, Jesus Christ said we cannot serve two masters.

Luke 16:13 - "No servant can serve two masters; for either he will hate the one and love the other, or he will be devoted to the one and despise the other. You cannot serve God and mammon" (**RSV**).

We will love one and hate the other. We cannot serve God and ourselves. Jesus warned all of us with these words in **Matthew 7**.

Matthew 7:21 - "Not every one that saith unto me, Lord, Lord, shall enter into the kingdom of heaven; but he that doeth the will of my Father which is in heaven" (**KJV**).

How do we do God's will?

We do God's will by seeking God and obeying God. Seeking God means asking God His will and seeking to know Him better in a relationship with Him. Obeying God is choosing to do God's will and not your own.

Are we Saved by Works? Absolutely Not!

If you believe in Jesus Christ and make Him your Savior and Lord (see how at the end), your sins are paid for by Jesus Christ's sinless blood. Trying to pay for what He paid for is wrong and cannot be done.

Galatians 2:16 says, "Knowing that a man is not justified by the works of the law, but by the faith of Jesus Christ, even we have believed in Jesus Christ, that we might be justified by the faith of Christ, and not by the works of the law: for by the works of the law shall no flesh be justified" (**KJV**).

Ephesians 2:8-9 - "For by grace are ye saved through faith; and that not of yourselves: it is the gift of God: Not of works, lest any man should boast" (**KJV**).

Titus 3:5-6 - "Not by works of righteousness which we have done, but according to his mercy he saved us, by the washing of regeneration, and renewing of the Holy Ghost; Which he shed on us abundantly through Jesus Christ our Saviour" (**KJV**).

Romans 3:28 - "Therefore we conclude that a man is justified by faith without the deeds of the law" (**KJV**).

Why is doing our own will so wrong?

If we do our own will, and not God's will, we are making ourselves and our own interests idols (or gods). God said that all idolaters (worshippers of idols or false gods) shall be cast into "the lake which burneth with fire and brimstone: which is the second death" (**Revelation 21:8, KJV**).

Revelation 21:7-8 - "He that overcometh shall inherit all things; and I will be his God, and he shall be my son. But the fearful, and unbelieving, and the abominable, and murderers, and whoremongers, and sorcerers, and idolaters, and all liars, shall have their part in the lake which burneth with fire and brimstone: which is the second death" (**KJV**).

Jesus Christ says this in:

Revelation 3:5 - "He that overcometh, the same shall be clothed in white raiment; and I will not blot out his name out of the book of life, but I will confess his name before my Father, and before his angels" (**KJV**).

If Jesus will not blot out the name of those who overcome, what will He do to those who refuse to seek Him and do His will? The need today is to seek God and to know Him deeply, and personally.

The love of money is the root of all evil.

CHAPTER 5

THE NEW VIRTUES

The Bible warns of 'perilous times' during the last days and so they are. The values which built civilization as it has been known for the last 4000 or so years will be rejected and exchanged for those which tear down families, God and life itself.

II Timothy 3:1 - "This know also, that in the last days perilous times shall come" (**KJV**).

One of the reasons for peril is the world will offer virtues which are not. They sound good but, upon closer inspection, are selfish, man-centered, anti-Christ ones. Concepts such as SIN, FEAR of GOD, FAITH, PATIENCE, SELFLESSNESS, SALVATION, RIGHTEOUSNESS and CHARITY are being exchanged and diluted for the world's weak tea of:

- Tolerance (of sin)
- Love (of approved attitudes only)
- Freedom (from the commandments of God)
- Liberty (from anything which restricts an individual's choices)

- Self-expression (celebration of self and the elevation of self as the highest standard of moral validation Open-mindedness (concerning wickedness)
- Choice (of evils)

Murder no longer is called murder. It takes on different names. Murder becomes "choice." Murder becomes "death with dignity." Murder becomes "mercy." Love is no longer love. Obsession, enslavement, compulsion, passion, addiction, infatuation, lust, mania, jealousy: all are labeled "love'. These new virtues are exalted by the world and placed above all others. Anyone with competing values will be labeled "old fashioned," shouted down or worse (Jameson, 2016).

Jesus? What? Don't push your superstitions on me! This is 2019! Nobody's gonna tell me what to do! I'm the master of my own destiny! In some cases, pleasures have been substituted for virtues. One example is the transformation of the appreciation of one's family (a natural state and a pleasure) into a virtue. Another is changing the companionship of a pet (a pleasure) into a virtue. Though values have rapidly changed, the new virtues have appropriated the names of the old.

Again, this is especially noticeable in what the world now calls "love." Real love is SELFLESS and concerned with the other person's well-being ahead of one's self. The world's new version of love emphasizes self, self and more self. Many younger folks believe love has to do with control: either gaining or surrendering it. This exchange of social values only gets worse and the meaning of words is being turned completely upside down (Jameson, 2016).

Hate becomes LOVE; LOVE of God Almighty becomes hate.

Isaiah 5:20 - "Woe unto them that call evil good, and good evil; that put darkness for light, and light for darkness; that put bitter for sweet, and sweet for bitter" (**KJV**)!

The New Virtues are lies. And such lies have a very short shelf-life. Is the reader already under the influence of the New Virtues? Is he calling good evil, and evil good? How can the reader tell? It is not yet too late to change.

Time is Running Out: Today is the Day of Salvation

I Corinthians 15:1-8 - "Moreover, brethren, I declare unto you the gospel which I preached unto you, which also ye have received, and wherein ye stand; By which also ye are saved, if ye keep in memory what I preached unto you, unless ye have believed in vain. For I delivered unto you first of all that which I also received, how that Christ died for our sins according to the scriptures; And that he was buried, and that he rose again the third day according to the scriptures: And that he was seen of Cephas, then of the twelve: After that, he was seen of above five hundred brethren at once; of whom the greater part remain unto this present, but some are fallen asleep. After that, he was seen of James; then of all the apostles. And last of all he was seen of me also, as of one born out of due time" **(KJV)**.

II Corinthians 4:3 - "But if our gospel be hid, it is hid to them that are lost" **(KJV)**.

The devil has many tricks, but one of his most insidious is to lull people into believing they have all the time in the world. For some of the lost, they have put off deciding for their salvation because "they aren't ready yet." To all who have such a cavalier attitude toward the free gift of eternal life: you may need that free gift before you realize. No one knows when their appointed time will come around. The Bible declares that all have an appointed time to die, and when that time comes, it is time it face judgment.

"This know also, that in the last days
perilous times shall come"

CHAPTER 6

FINDING YOUR MORAL COMPASS

In this polarized political climate, people are vocal about their perceptions of right and wrong. What might appear to be simple, has become complex. The values we hold are, in part, offered up by the adults who raised us, by the culture in which we were entrenched and by our willingness to learn and adapt to new ideas that come our way.

In a world with so many diverse beliefs and values, how do you determine right from wrong? I know someone who believes that there is no such thing, and that we should just honor people's feelings. That doesn't sit right with me. What if I feel like taking something that doesn't belong to me or spew hatred because someone is different from me or strike someone because I am angry with them? I was taught that those were in the no-no category. In this case, morality seems absolute and not relative (Weinstein, 2018).

An article published in Greater Good Magazine, states, "a recent Gallop Poll indicates that nearly 80 percent of Americans rated the overall state of morality in the United States as fair or poor. Even more troubling is the widely held opinion that people are becoming more selfish and dishonest. According to that same Gallup Poll, 77 percent of Americans believe that the state of moral values is getting worse. "One place in which values and morals are considered fodder for conversation is in the business world. Is it acceptable to take credit for a colleague's work? Is it permissible to pilfer office supplies from your employer? Is it okay to take extra change from the cash register or food from the pantry where you work?

A principle known as Kohlberg's Stages of Moral Development sets the stage for our understanding of what is right and wrong. It is broken down into concepts that guide decision making as we mature. One of the landmark cases that Kohlberg put forth was called Heinz Dilemma, which describes a man who steals a drug that his wife needs to survive, from the inventor who is overcharging by 100% and won't allow the man to pay less. I recall hearing about this while in graduate school and it tested my own moral sensibilities. I can feel when someone or something resonates with me. Then when someone doesn't with my beliefs I let them go. Surrender the idea that I am in charge of anyone or anything. Compassion seems to follow. "Does it feel right? Are your actions or decisions helping or hurting, I believe we all know deep in our soul right from wrong" (Weinstein, 2018).

The golden rule: don't do anything that you wouldn't want someone to do to you. Doesn't mean it's wrong or right, that is determined by each person, their experience, their perspective. And of course, we have laws. They pretty much cover it. Outside of that, we model better behavior and hope evolution takes care of the rest. Some things in life are indeed black and white and are indeed objectively right or wrong. Lots of things in life are gray, and leeway in considering another person's opinion/feeling/ belief is appropriate. But moral relativism only goes so far. To say that there is no right or wrong 'and that we should just honor people's feelings' is emotionally lazy and shows a lack of integrity.

"One way to frame such things is in light of what works and what doesn't. In this light, to behave without integrity is not wrong, however, it does have a cost. When integrity is out agreements don't work when agreements are not reliable, possibilities are limited." "It's all about tolerance and not hurting others. If your religion teaches peace, love and respect then it should be celebrated. There is no place for hatred, bigotry and extremism" (Weinstein, 2018).

"Some things are universal. I know of no culture, religion or philosophy that condones theft or violence, at least on the individual level. They all seem to condone such things when done by the State though." "I believe that in healthy humans there is an inner compass that guides right from wrong. It may get modified through various lenses of philosophy, religion, and culture, but I think seeking peace and integrity and not causing harm are pretty universal. Unfortunately, it is also possible to get estranged from that compass, so it is good to stay in balance and in touch with it as much as we can."

"Wrong does not cease to be wrong
because the majority share in it."

CHAPTER 7

HOW DO CHILDREN LEARN RIGHT FROM WRONG?

Little ones want what they want, and they like to be in charge of themselves. But they also depend on us, the parents who care for them, and they trust us to have their best interests at heart. They may not always do what we say, but they will always, eventually, do what we do. So most of what children learn about how to behave is from what we model. That's why, regardless of what you consciously teach your child, he will learn what he lives (Markham, 2017).

Let's think about how children learn right from wrong (Markham, 2017).

- When we cheerfully help them clean up the spilled milk, they learn that it isn't an emergency, so they don't need to cry or to blame, and can simply solve the problem.
- When we offer understanding as we say no to their requests, they learn that they won't always get what they want, but they get something better — a mom or dad who always understands.
- When we're there to listen, they learn that life can be tough, but they can always recover and find a better way.

- When we delight in them, they learn that they're of value.
- When we're forgiving of their mistakes, they learn that no one's perfect— but they're more than enough just the way they are.
- When we apologize and make amends, they learn how to repair the damage they do.
- When we try to see their side of things, they try to see our side of things.
- When we believe in their best intentions even when they aren't at their best, they don't want to disappoint us.
- When we're clear about the limits, and give them support to meet those limits, they try hard to meet our expectations.
- When we're compassionate in the face of their upsets, they learn that emotions aren't an emergency and can be managed.
- When we model the emotional regulation and responsible behavior we want from our child, we raise a child we can be proud of.
- When we share with them, heart to heart and without blame, that the dog is hungry because they forgot to feed him, they learn that they never want to hurt a helpless creature again.
- When we help them come up with a system to remind themselves to feed the dog so they don't forget in the future, they learn to manage themselves.
- When we punish them for forgetting to feed the dog, they get angry at us and at the dog, which doesn't motivate them to want to care for him.
- When we scream at them, they learn that tantrums are ok, and they learn to scream at us.
- When we punish them, they learn that's how to solve problems, people with more power are allowed to use it against people with less power.
- When we swear at another driver, they learn incivility, not to mention some embarrassing words.

- When we lie to someone on the phone when they're listening, they learn that dishonesty is ok.

- When we lie about their age to get them into an amusement park, they learn that cheating is ok.

- When we speed in the car, they learn that breaking the law is ok if we don't get caught.

- When we promise to play a game with them and then renege, they learn that promises can be broken.

- When we ignore the feelings that drove their behavior, they learn that there's no one to help them with the big scary feelings that pop out and pressure them to "do bad."

- When we spank them, they learn that bigger people are allowed to hit smaller people.

- When we punish them, they learn that they're bad people — bad for doing wrong, bad for having the bad feelings that made them do wrong, bad for being mad at us for punishing them, and bad because they know they won't be able to stop themselves from doing it again.

Children don't learn right from wrong by being punished, any more than they learn red from blue by being punished. Kids learn when we show them red, and also when we show them kindness, responsibility, generosity, honesty, compassion, and all the other things we want them to learn, in action, every day. When children feel close to their parents, they want to "follow" them. Going against their parents would be going against the most important people in their lives. That's why connection is 90% of parenting. Until the child feels the connection, she isn't open to our direction. Of course, the prefrontal cortex that can keep strong emotions in check to help your child behave is still developing until age 25, so your child won't always make the right choice. But if you're parenting with loving guidance, at least she'll be more likely to WANT to make the right choice (Markham, 2017).

Do you have to be perfect? No, of course not. But then you can't expect your child to be perfect, either. Modeling self-forgiveness and making amends with those you love is part of teaching your child to repair the inevitable small ruptures that happen between humans, even when we love each other. It's part of how you keep your child connected and wanting to "do right."

They learn what they live!

CHAPTER 8

RIGHT AND WRONG

According to one author, we've seriously lost our way. He says we are like men adrift at sea without a compass. As a result, moral dilemmas plague us as we look ahead to the 21st century. Something has gone terribly wrong. Many of us know it, but what to do about it evades us. Is there any way to know the difference between right and wrong? Does religion have anything left to offer? From time to time we hear that the established churches are in confusion, that too often their leaders have nothing to say that's practical and helpful. Where does the truth on these matters lie (Hulme, 2000)?

Back in the days just before the Second World War, things were different. The Western world was dominated by a particular value system. In a book titled *1938: A World Vanishing*, Brian Cleeve wrote about the difference between Britain as it was entering the war and the way it had become about 50 years later. He said: "There really was, as nostalgia remembers, an air of greater contentment. Of a sturdier confidence in the future. People had a greater stock of moral certainties. Right and wrong were not matters for debate." Since then much has changed, of course. Now right and wrong are matters for debate.

The end of the Second World War was a turning point. And while the morality of the '30s was not perfect, Cleeve noted that "to exchange a false morality for no morality at all is not necessarily an exchange for the better. And if, as a survivor of pre-war years, I were to offer an opinion as to one difference between then and now that is for the worse, I would have to choose morality, the morality of believing that there are real and objective standards of behavior, that there are such things as virtues, and such things as vices; that certain things are unarguably good, and others unarguably bad." What has happened in contemporary Western society is the promotion of democratic ideas beyond reason. It's often been noted that democracy carries within itself the seeds of its own destruction (Hulme, 2000).

> **"In our modern eagerness to be tolerant,**
> **we have come to tolerate things which**
> **no society can tolerate and remain healthy."**

"In our modern eagerness to be tolerant," Cleeve stated, "we have come to tolerate things which no society can tolerate and remain healthy. In our understandable anxiety not to set ourselves up as judges, we have come to believe that all judgments are wrong. In our revulsion against hypocrisy and false morality we have abandoned morality itself. And with modest hesitations but firm convictions I submit that this has not made us happier, but much unhappier. We are like men at sea without a compass" (Hulme, 2000).

He continued: "In 1938 in Britain the average man and woman still possessed a keen notion of what was right and what was wrong, in his and her own personal life, in the community, and in the world at large. When the war was finally begun it was clearly and rightly seen as a moral war by the ordinary people who were being called on to risk their lives in it" (Hulme, 2000)

Has the time arrived again when ordinary people must make moral standards a personal crusade? Has the time come to stand up and be counted for the difference between right and wrong? We all know what's been going on around the world. Our leaders have been unable to stem the flow of violence, the corruption and the many evils of modern life. Why? Could it be that the answers do not lie with leaders and they are found somewhere else, such as in the realm of personal responsibility? There was a time in the Western world when we could recite the Ten Commandments. They were taught in school. There was a time when our parents led the way in disciplining us for bad behavior.

Much of our morality was based on
the Book of books, the Bible.

The BIBLE is more than a piece of great literature.

Are moral standards in the eye of the beholder?

CHAPTER 9

RIGHT VS. WRONG

How do we know what is right and what is wrong? How do we base decisions on the grey areas of life from the Bible? The Bible doesn't address each and every issue of life so how can we find out what God would have us do in areas of right and wrong and know that we are making the right decision?

Knowing Right from Wrong from the Bible

The Bible does not cover each and every issue in the Christian's walk and so we must use wisdom to discern the will of God and whether something is right or something is wrong. If we can understand the basic principles laid down by God Almighty, then we can know whether something is right or whether something is wrong. For example, the Bible does not say that abortion is wrong precisely, but we know that God formed us in the womb and calls us by name before we are born (Wellman, 2012).

Jeremiah 1:5 - "Before I formed you in the womb I knew you, and before you were born I consecrated you; I appointed you a prophet to the nations" **(RSV)**.

And we also know that God is the giver of life and is the only one who has the right to take life.

Exodus 20:13 - "You shall not kill" (**RSV**).

By our knowing these facts we understand that God is pro-life and the fact that our days are numbered by Him shows that He alone decides when a human being should die.

Job 14:5 - "Since his days are determined, and the number of his months is with thee, and thou hast appointed his bounds that he cannot pass" (**RSV**).

There was a "No Swimming" sign up at a sand pit many years ago but there were some children swimming in this pond. They were disobeying the sign. That sign was posted because there was a sink hole in it and so it was a danger for anyone to swim in it. One of the children began to flounder in the water and began to drown. Now, we know that we are to obey those in authority in **Romans 13**, but we also know that God wants us to take a higher principle when a human life is at stake. So should a person disobey the "No Swimming" sign and not save the child from drowning? Of course not! (Wellman, 2012).

The point is that someone saved the young child from drowning and had to instantly discern that the value of the human life was of infinitely higher value than disobedience to the "No Swimming" sign. Now if the children had obeyed the sign in the first place, they might not have nearly drowned.

The same principle applies to trying to find what is right and what is wrong where the Bible is silent.

The Bible doesn't say, "You shall wear seat belts" but since we understand that we are to obey those who are the governing authorities we *should* wear our seat belts because it's the law and it's a known scientific fact that seat belts save lives (Wellman, 2012).

Romans 13:1-3 - "Let every person be subject to the governing authorities. For there is no authority except from God, and those that exist have been instituted by God. Therefore he who resists the authorities resists what God has appointed, and those who resist will incur judgment. For rulers are not a terror to good conduct, but to bad. Would you have no fear of him who is in authority? Then do what is good, and you will receive his approval" (**RSV**).

Biblical Answers of Right and Wrong

If someone asks you what the Bible says about gambling, you can not find a specific answer about this in the Scriptures per say, but you can find Scriptures about loving money more than God.

II Timothy 3:2 - "People will be lovers of themselves, lovers of money, boastful, proud, abusive, disobedient to their parents, ungrateful, unholy" (**NIV**).

About greed?

I Timothy 6:9 - "Those who want to get rich fall into temptation and a trap and into many foolish and harmful desires that plunge people into ruin and destruction" (**NIV**).

About coveting?

Exodus 20:17 - "You shall not covet your neighbor's house. You shall not covet your neighbor's wife, or his male or female servant, his ox or donkey, or anything that belongs to your neighbor" (**NIV**).

And about storing up treasures on earth instead of in heaven.

Matthew 6:19 - "Do not store up for yourselves treasures on earth, where moths and vermin destroy, and where thieves break in and steal" (**NIV**).

For example:

Proverbs 10:22 says, "The blessing of the LORD brings wealth, without painful toil for it" (**NIV**).

When we want to know whether something is right or wrong, we simply have to consult the Bible in areas where the question lies. Should a Christian vote or not or should a believer run for political office? That is a question that I have heard many times and the Bible appears to be silent in this area, but if we look closely at Paul's teaching on how a Christian should live in society we can turn to (Wellman, 2012).

Romans 13:1 says, "Let everyone be subject to the governing authorities, for there is no authority except that which God has established. The authorities that exist have been established by God" (**NIV**).

Every citizen has a legal right to vote so we are more than free to not only vote but to participate in running for office. Why? Because "The authorities that exist have been established by God." If someone complains about the politician and yet doesn't vote, then they have no excuse because they could have voted for someone else or they could have voted for someone in the first place if they chose not to vote that is.

Another example is that we can know with certainty that we should not cheat on our taxes by reading:

Romans 13:6-7 - "This is also why you pay taxes, for the authorities are God's servants, who give their full time to governing. Give to everyone what you owe them: If you owe taxes, pay taxes; if revenue, then revenue; if respect, then respect; if honor, then honor" (**NIV**).

We must pay our taxes and pay what is our fair share because "the authorities are God's servants, who give their full time to governing." To decide if we should drive just over the speed limit or not:

Romans 13:3-5 is very clear, "For rulers hold no terror for those who do right, but for those who do wrong. Do you want to be free from fear of the one in authority? Then do what is right and you will be commended. For the one in authority is God's servant for your good. But if you do wrong, be afraid, for rulers do not bear the sword for no reason. They are God's servants, agents of wrath to bring punishment on the wrongdoer.

Therefore, it is necessary to submit to the authorities, not only because of possible punishment but also as a matter of conscience" (**NIV**).

You don't need to be nervous looking in your rear view mirror if you see a police car coming and you are doing the speed limit, "for those who do right" but if you're speeding, "be afraid, for rulers do not bear the sword for no reason."

> Father,
> I am so tired of pursuing folly and I'm
> Sick and tired of being sick and tired.
> I have felt so hopeless and lost.
> My heart is filled with despair.
> I have believed lies and accepted disillusionment
> As my lot in life, rather than embracing Your path.
> I have foolishly believed in the ways of those
> Who have mocked Your Holy Name.
> Forgive me for being so willful
> For believing the deception of those
> Who pursue the road to destruction.
> This isn't what I want for my future,
> Not for me or for anybody I know,
> But it seems to be all I am capable of producing.
> I need Your help not some time in the future
> Father, but right here and right now.
> Will You help me this very minute?
> All I have to offer is my broken heart
> And my willingness to mend my ways.
> Thank You, Father,
> Amen.

The heart and soul of America has become flawed. Fools are leading us. Corruption abounds. It has become so commonplace that there isn't much of an attempt to hide it. Being desensitized, we have come to expect political graft and fraud as par for the course, believing every political leader is the same way. Shrugging our collective shoulders, we say, "This is just the way things are, and it is not going to change."

There is a Scripture that says, "Without a vision, the people perish." This can also mean, "The people are unrestrained." In America, I believe the second interpretation is the most accurate. We are unrestrained. We champion wrong, calling it right, while legislating Evil and calling it Good. Everyone does what is right in his or her eyes, all at the expense of the nation's corporate soul.

We must return to the ways of our forefathers,
including their beliefs,
which were noble and high-minded
and BIBLE based.

CHAPTER 10

ETHICS TAUGHT OR NOT?

Afundamental part of personality that defines behavior and the way person reacts or perceives things is 'ethic'. Ethics like education always remain with you as a very significant part of your character. Ethics is a Greek word that means character or manners. But unfortunately it is collapsing in each and every sphere of life, so teaching this fundamental way of life is the need of an hour. Unethical practices may lead to major disasters. Increasing crime forced us to think if we are left with any moral values and ethics. There is no industry that is untouched by unethical practices. So it is highly important to teach importance of ethics. Deteriorating value system laid further stress on this (Hattangadi, 2014).

Christian ethics is well summarized by **Colossians 3:1-6** - "Since, then, you have been raised with Christ, set your hearts on things above, where Christ is seated at the right hand of God. Set your minds on things above, not on earthly things. For you died, and your life is now hidden with Christ in God. When Christ, who is your life, appears, then you also will appear with him in glory. Put to death, therefore, whatever belongs to your earthly nature: sexual immorality, impurity, lust, evil desires and greed, which is idolatry. Because of these, the wrath of God is coming" (**NIV**).

Science defines ethics as "a set of moral principles, the study of morality." Therefore, Christian ethics would be the principles derived from the Christian faith by which we act. While God's Word may not cover every situation we face throughout our lives, its principles give us the standards by which we must conduct ourselves in those situations where there are no explicit instructions.

While more than just a list of "do's" and "don'ts," the Bible does give us detailed instructions on how we should live. The Bible is all we need to know about how to live the Christian life. However, the Bible does not explicitly cover every situation we will face in our lives. How then is it sufficient for the all the ethical dilemmas we face? That is where Christian ethics comes in.

For example, the Bible does not say anything explicitly about the use of illegal drugs, yet based on the principles we learn through Scripture, we can know that it is wrong. For one thing, the Bible tells us that the body is a temple of the Holy Spirit and that we should honor God with it.

I Corinthians 6:19-20 - "What? know ye not that your body is the temple of the Holy Ghost which is in you, which ye have of God, and ye are not your own? For ye are bought with a price: therefore glorify God in your body, and in your spirit, which are God's" (**KJV**).

Knowing what drugs do to our bodies, the harm they cause to various organs—we know that by using them we would be destroying the temple of the Holy Spirit. That is certainly not honoring to God. The Bible also tells us that we are to follow the authorities that God Himself has put into place:

Romans 13:1 - "Let every soul be subject unto the higher powers. For there is no power but of God: the powers that be are ordained of God" (**KJV**).

Given the illegal nature of the drugs, by using them we are not submitting to the authorities but are rebelling against them. Does this mean if illegal drugs were legalized it would be ok? Not without violating the first principle.

By using the principles we find in Scripture, Christians can determine the ethical course for any given situation. In some cases it will be simple, like the rules for Christian living we find in Colossians, chapter 3. In other cases, however, we need to do a little digging. The best way to do that is to pray over God's Word. The Holy Spirit indwells every believer, and part of His role is teaching us how to live: "But the Counselor, the Holy Spirit, whom the Father will send in my name, will teach you all things and will remind you of everything I have said to you".

John 14:26 - "But the Comforter, which is the Holy Ghost, whom the Father will send in my name, he shall teach you all things, and bring all things to your remembrance, whatsoever I have said unto you" (**KJV**).

I John 2:27 - "But the anointing which ye have received of him abideth in you, and ye need not that any man teach you: but as the same anointing teacheth you of all things, and is truth, and is no lie, and even as it hath taught you, ye shall abide in him" (**KJV**).

So, when we pray over Scripture, the Spirit will guide us and teach us. He will show us the principles we need to stand on for any given situation. While God's Word does not cover every situation we will face in our lives, it is all-sufficient for living a Christian life. For most things, we can simply see what the Bible says and follow the proper course based on that. In ethical questions where Scripture does not give explicit instructions, we need to look for principles that can be applied to the situation. We must pray over His Word, and open ourselves to His Spirit. The Spirit will teach us and guide us through the Bible to find the principles on which we need to stand so we may live as a Christian should.

The Spirit will guide us and teach us!

CHAPTER 11

WHY DO THEY CALL GOOD EVIL AND EVIL GOOD?

Evil worms its way into our lives by presenting a harmless appearance, such as the full-page, full-color ads of "the man of distinction," dressed impeccably, sipping a glass of whiskey with his friends in the warmth of a well-appointed room. Such ads say nothing of the new alcoholics that are being made every day, nor of the problem of excessive drinking that is eating at the heart of our civilization. Of course it wouldn't be in good taste to show a picture of a "man of distinction" on Skid Row who began his drinking on Fifth Avenue but is ending it in the Bowery. It wouldn't be in good taste, but it would be honest (Smith, 2017).

Romans 8:6-7 - "For to be carnally minded is death; but to be spiritually minded is life and peace. Because the carnal mind is enmity against God: for it is not subject to the law of God, neither indeed can be" (**KJV**).

If we do not seek God, we will be depending on our own carnal mind, which is "enmity against God" and at war with God. Evil men will not seek God.

Psalm 10:4 says, "The wicked, through the pride of his countenance, will not seek after God: God is not in all his thoughts" (**KJV**).

Evil men call good evil and evil good because they are not seeking God and are depending instead on their own carnal mind. Depending on your own will instead of on God's will is a type of rebellion.

Luke 16:13 says, "No servant can serve two masters: for either he will hate the one, and love the other; or else he will hold to the one, and despise the other. Ye cannot serve God and mammon" (**KJV**).

Mammon is money and the love of money is the root of all evil.

I Timothy 6:10 - "For the love of money is the root of all evil: which while some coveted after, they have erred from the faith, and pierced themselves through with many sorrows" (**KJV**).

If we do our own will we are not serving God, but we are serving ourselves. We can't do both. If you serve yourself (and thus love the world) you cannot love God or be filled with God's love

I John 2:15-17 - "Love not the world, neither the things that are in the world. If any man love the world, the love of the Father is not in him. For all that is in the world, the lust of the flesh, and the lust of the eyes, and the pride of life, is not of the Father, but is of the world. And the world passeth away, and the lust thereof: but he that doeth the will of God abideth for ever" (**KJV**).

In **Mark 9**, Jesus Christ said to remove what causes you to sin (or be offended) lest you be cast into Hell.

Mark 9:47-48 - "And if thine eye offend thee, pluck it out: it is better for thee to enter into the kingdom of God with one eye, than having two eyes to be cast into hell fire: Where their worm dieth not, and the fire is not quenched" (**KJV**).

Sin can lead to spiritual separation in Hell (death).

Romans 6:16 says, "Know ye not, that to whom ye yield yourselves servants to obey, his servants ye are to whom ye obey; whether of sin unto death, or of obedience unto righteousness" (**KJV**)?

We need to deny ourselves, take up our cross, and follow Jesus. Jesus Christ told us to do this in:

Mark 8:34-35 - "And he called to him the multitude with his disciples, and said to them, "If any man would come after me, let him deny himself and take up his cross and follow me. For whoever would save his life will lose it; and whoever loses his life for my sake and the gospel's will save it" (**RSV**).

Verse 35 tells us that we need to lose our lives, our pursuits, goals, and fleshly desires which are apart from God's will. If we chose our own will over God's will, God is then not the one we are serving. We would be serving ourselves instead of God. Remember, Jesus Christ said we cannot serve two masters.

Luke 16:13 - "No servant can serve two masters; for either he will hate the one and love the other, or he will be devoted to the one and despise the other. You cannot serve God and mammon" (**RSV**).

We will love one and hate the other. We cannot serve God and ourselves. Jesus warned all of us with these words in **Matthew 7**.

Matthew 7:21 - "Not every one that saith unto me, Lord, Lord, shall enter into the kingdom of heaven; but he that doeth the will of my Father which is in heaven" (**KJV**).

How do we do God's will?

We do God's will by seeking God and obeying God. Seeking God means asking God His will and seeking to know Him better in a relationship with Him. Obeying God is choosing to do God's will and not your own.

Are we Saved by Works? Absolutely Not!

If you believe in Jesus Christ and make Him your Savior and Lord (see how at the end), your sins are paid for by Jesus Christ's sinless blood. Trying to pay for what He paid for is wrong and cannot be done.

Galatians 2:16 says, "Knowing that a man is not justified by the works of the law, but by the faith of Jesus Christ, even we have believed in Jesus Christ, that we might be justified by the faith of Christ, and not by the works of the law: for by the works of the law shall no flesh be justified" (**KJV**).

Ephesians 2:8-9 - "For by grace are ye saved through faith; and that not of yourselves: it is the gift of God: Not of works, lest any man should boast" (**KJV**).

Titus 3:5-6 - "Not by works of righteousness which we have done, but according to his mercy he saved us, by the washing of regeneration, and renewing of the Holy Ghost; Which he shed on us abundantly through Jesus Christ our Saviour" (**KJV**).

Romans 3:28 - "Therefore we conclude that a man is justified by faith without the deeds of the law" (**KJV**).

Why is doing our own will so wrong?

If we do our own will, and not God's will, we are making ourselves and our own interests idols (or gods). God said that all idolaters (worshippers of idols or false gods) shall be cast into "the lake which burneth with fire and brimstone: which is the second death" (**Revelation 21:8, KJV**).

Revelation 21:7-8 - "He that overcometh shall inherit all things; and I will be his God, and he shall be my son. But the fearful, and unbelieving, and the abominable, and murderers, and whoremongers, and sorcerers, and idolaters, and all liars, shall have their part in the lake which burneth with fire and brimstone: which is the second death" (**KJV**).

Jesus Christ says this in:

Revelation 3:5 - "He that overcometh, the same shall be clothed in white raiment; and I will not blot out his name out of the book of life, but I will confess his name before my Father, and before his angels" (**KJV**).

If Jesus will not blot out the name of those who overcome, what will He do to those who refuse to seek Him and do His will? The need today is to seek God and to know Him deeply, and personally.

No servant can serve two masters!

CHAPTER 12

DEFINITION OF EVIL?

E vil is usually thought of as that which is morally wrong, sinful, or wicked; however, the word evil can also refer to anything that causes harm, with or without the moral dimension. The word is used both ways in the Bible. Anything that contradicts the holy nature of God is evil.

Psalm 51:4 - "Against thee, thee only, have I sinned, and done this evil in thy sight: that thou mightest be justified when thou speakest, and be clear when thou judgest" (**KJV**).

On the flip side, any disaster, tragedy, or calamity can also be called an "evil" event.

I Kings 17:20 - "And he cried unto the Lord, and said, O Lord my God, hast thou also brought evil upon the widow with whom I sojourn, by slaying her son" (**KJV**)?

Evil behavior includes sin committed against other people (murder, theft, adultery) and evil committed against God (unbelief, idolatry, blasphemy). From the disobedience in the Garden of Eden:

Genesis 2:9 - "And out of the ground made the Lord God to grow every tree that is pleasant to the sight, and good for food; the tree of life also in the midst of the garden, and the tree of knowledge of good and evil" (**KJV**).

To the wickedness of Babylon the Great:

Revelation 18:2 - "And he cried mightily with a strong voice, saying, Babylon the great is fallen, is fallen, and is become the habitation of devils, and the hold of every foul spirit, and a cage of every unclean and hateful bird" (**KJV**).

The Bible speaks of the fact of evil, and man is held responsible for the evil he commits:

Ezekiel 18:20 - "The soul that sinneth, it shall die. The son shall not bear the iniquity of the father, neither shall the father bear the iniquity of the son: the righteousness of the righteous shall be upon him, and the wickedness of the wicked shall be upon him" (**KJV**).

Essentially, evil is a lack of goodness. Moral evil is not a physical thing; it is a lack or privation of a good thing. As Christian philosopher J. P. Moreland has noted, "Evil is a lack of goodness. It is goodness spoiled. You can have good without evil, but you cannot have evil without good." Or as Christian apologist Greg Koukl has said, "Human freedom was used in such a way as to diminish goodness in the world, and that diminution, that lack of goodness, that is what we call evil." And he cried mightily with a strong voice, saying, Babylon the great is fallen, is fallen, and is become the habitation of devils, and the hold of every foul spirit, and a cage of every unclean and hateful bird (Romig, 2012).

God is love.

I John 4:8 - "He that loveth not knoweth not God; for God is love" (**KJV**).

The absence of love in a person is un-God-like and therefore evil. And an absence of love manifests itself in unloving behavior. The same can be said concerning God's mercy, justice, patience, etc. The lack of these godly qualities in anyone constitutes evil. That evil then manifests itself in behavior that is unmerciful, unjust, impatient, etc., bringing more harm into the good world that God has made. As it turns out, we lack a lot: "As it is written, 'There is no one righteous, not even one'".

Romans 3:10 - "As it is written, There is none righteous, no, not one" (**KJV**).

Moral evil is wrong done to others, and it can exist even when unaccompanied by external action. Murder is an evil action, but it has its start with the moral evil of hatred in the heart.

Matthew 5:21-22 - "Ye have heard that it was said of them of old time, Thou shalt not kill; and whosoever shall kill shall be in danger of the judgment: But I say unto you, That whosoever is angry with his brother without a cause shall be in danger of the judgment: and whosoever shall say to his brother, Raca, shall be in danger of the council: but whosoever shall say, Thou fool, shall be in danger of hell fire" (**KJV**).

Committing adultery is evil, but so is the moral evil of lust in the heart.

Matthew 5:27 - "Ye have heard that it was said by them of old time, Thou shalt not commit adultery" (**KJV**).

Jesus said, "What comes out of a person is what defiles them. For it is from within, out of a person's heart, that evil thoughts come, sexual immorality, theft, murder, adultery, greed, malice, deceit, lewdness, envy, slander, arrogance and folly. All these evils come from inside and defile a person"

Mark 7:20-23 - "And he said, That which cometh out of the man, that defileth the man. For from within, out of the heart of men, proceed evil thoughts, adulteries, fornications, murders, Thefts, covetousness, wickedness, deceit, lasciviousness, an evil eye, blasphemy, pride, foolishness: All these evil things come from within, and defile the man" (**KJV**).

Those who fall into evil behavior usually start slowly. Paul shows the tragic progression into more and more evil in **Romans 1**. It starts with refusing to glorify God or give thanks to Him.

Romans 1:21 - "Because that, when they knew God, they glorified him not as God, neither were thankful; but became vain in their imaginations, and their foolish heart was darkened" (**KJV**).

And it ends with God giving them over to a "depraved mind" and allowing them to be "filled with every kind of wickedness" (**verses 28–29**).

Those who:

Mark 7:20-23 - "And he said, That which cometh out of the man, that defileth the man. For from within, out of the heart of men, proceed evil thoughts, adulteries, fornications, murders, Thefts, covetousness, wickedness, deceit, lasciviousness, an evil eye, blasphemy, pride, foolishness: All these evil things come from within, and defile the man" (**KJV**).

Practice evil are in Satan's trap and are slaves to sin: "Opponents of the Lord's servant must be gently instructed, in the hope that God will grant them repentance leading them to a knowledge of the truth, and that they will come to their senses and escape from the trap of the devil, who has taken them captive to do his will" (Romig, 2012).

II Timothy 2:25-26 - "In meekness instructing those that oppose themselves; if God peradventure will give them repentance to the acknowledging of the truth; And that they may recover themselves out of the snare of the devil, who are taken captive by him at his will" (**KJV**).

John 8:34 - "Jesus answered them, Verily, verily, I say unto you, Whosoever committeth sin is the servant of sin" (**KJV**).

Only by the grace of God can we be set free.

Physical evil is the trouble that befalls people in the world, and it may or may not be linked to moral evil or divine judgment.

Ecclesiastes 11:2 - "Give a portion to seven, and also to eight; for thou knowest not what evil shall be upon the earth" (**KJV**).

Counsels us to diversify our investments, for this reason: "thou knowest not what evil shall be upon the earth". The word evil in this case means "disaster," "misfortune," or "calamity," and that's how other translations word it. Sometimes, physical evil is simply the result of an accident or causes unknown, with no known moral cause; examples would include injuries, car wrecks, hurricanes, and earthquakes. Other times, physical evil is God's retribution for the sins of an individual or group (Romig, 2012).

Sodom and the surrounding cities were destroyed for their sins Genesis 19, and God "made them an example of what is going to happen to the ungodly".

II Peter 2:6 - "And turning the cities of Sodom and Gomorrha into ashes condemned them with an overthrow, making them an example unto those that after should live ungodly" (**KJV**).

Many times, God warned Israel of the calamities that awaited them if they rebelled: "The LORD also is wise, and will bring evil, and will not call back his words: but will arise against the house of the evildoers, and against the help of them that work iniquity".

Isaiah 31:2 - "Yet he also is wise, and will bring evil, and will not call back his words: but will arise against the house of the evildoers, and against the help of them that work iniquity" (**KJV**).

In all cases, God works through the situation to bring about His good purpose:

Romans 8:28 - "And we know that all things work together for good to them that love God, to them who are the called according to his purpose" **(KJV)**.

God is not the author of moral evil; rather, it is His holiness that defines it. Created in God's image, we bear the responsibility to make moral choices that please God and conform to His will. He wills our sanctification:

I Thessalonians 4:3 - "For this is the will of God, even your sanctification, that ye should abstain from fornication" **(KJV)**.

And does not wish us to sin:

James 1:13 - "Let no man say when he is tempted, I am tempted of God: for God cannot be tempted with evil, neither tempteth he any man" **(KJV)**.

In repentance and faith in Christ, we have forgiveness of sin and a reversal of the moral evil within us.

Acts 3:19 - "Repent ye therefore, and be converted, that your sins may be blotted out, when the times of refreshing shall come from the presence of the Lord" **(KJV)**.

Romans 12:21 - "Be not overcome of evil, but overcome evil with good" **(KJV)**.

As God's children, we walk according to this command:

"Do not be overcome by evil, but
overcome evil with good".

CHAPTER 13

WHAT IS THE DIFFERENCE BETWEEN NATURAL EVIL AND MORAL EVIL?

Moral evil is evil that is caused by human activity. Murder, rape, robbery, embezzlement, hatred, jealousy, etc., are all moral evils. When people, created in the image of God, choose to act in defiance of God's law, the result is moral evil. Moral evil can also be linked to inaction to purposefully ignore a cry for help is a moral evil. Natural evil is that which causes pain and suffering to humanity but which is not due to direct human involvement. Congenital diseases, tsunamis, earthquakes, drought, and famine are all cases of natural evil. There is no morality involved in such events (Snoke, 2016).

The categories of natural and moral evil raise some interesting philosophical and theological questions. Some philosophers see natural evil as a real obstacle to belief in an omnipotent, benevolent God. They say that, if a human being did the kinds of things that God does (cause earthquakes, cancer, etc.), then that person would be morally evil. If it would be wrong for a human being to do these things, why are they not wrong for God?

The points below are offered specifically in response to the problem of natural evil:

- **God does not answer to us, but we must answer to Him.**

Romans 14:12 - "So then every one of us shall give account of himself to God" (**KJV**).

God alone holds the power of life and death. It would be wrong for a person to cause an earthquake that would kill thousands because human beings do not have that prerogative. God, on the other hand, does. He is the creator and giver of life, and He can withdraw that gift when, and in what manner, He chooses.

We have all sinned and deserve the death penalty:

Romans 3:23 - "For all have sinned, and come short of the glory of God" (**KJV**).

Romans 6:23 - "For the wages of sin is death; but the gift of God is eternal life through Jesus Christ our Lord" (**KJV**).

The fact that God allows any of us to live is a sign of His grace and forbearance.

- **Natural evil is a result of original human sin.**

Things are not the way they were created to be. With sin, pain and death entered into the system in Genesis chapter 3. Paul tells us that all of creation is currently suffering, waiting for the time when it is set free from "bondage to decay".

Romans 8:20-22 - "For the creature was made subject to vanity, not willingly, but by reason of him who hath subjected the same in hope, Because the creature itself also shall be delivered from the bondage of corruption into the glorious liberty of the children of God. For we know that the whole creation groaneth and travaileth in pain together until now" (**KJV**).

Broadly speaking, natural evil is God's judgment on humanity.

- **Natural evil is exacerbated by human sin.**

When there is a disaster, there are often many examples of people working and giving sacrificially and heroically in order to help alleviate suffering. Unfortunately, there will also be many examples of people looting, price gouging, hording supplies, and acting in selfish and cowardly ways to the detriment of those around them. The singular biggest cause of famine in the world today is not weather but displacement due to warfare. In these situations, food is often available for distribution to refugees, but it rots in warehouses while government officials argue over the distribution or use the opportunity to enrich themselves (Snoke, 2016).

The only hope for people in a world filled with evil (whether moral or natural) is Jesus Christ. He does not promise escape from the evil in this world. In fact, He promises that His followers will experience it.

John 16:33 - "These things I have spoken unto you, that in me ye might have peace. In the world ye shall have tribulation: but be of good cheer; I have overcome the world" (**KJV**).

He also promises that believers will have an inheritance in the and new heaven and new earth where there is no evil or suffering of any kind.

Revelation 21:1 - "And I saw a new heaven and a new earth: for the first heaven and the first earth were passed away; and there was no more sea" (**KJV**).

Revelation 21:4 - "And God shall wipe away all tears from their eyes; and there shall be no more death, neither sorrow, nor crying, neither shall there be any more pain: for the former things are passed away" (**KJV**).

The created order will be restored to its original balance, eliminating natural evil, and the people will be conformed to the image of Christ, eliminating moral evil.

Our HOPE is Jesus Christ!

CHAPTER 14

WHAT DOES THE BIBLE SAY ABOUT GOOD VERSUS EVIL?

Among the most universal beliefs across all humanity is the concept of "good versus evil." Every culture in every era has held to some version of this struggle. The definitions of the terms *good* and evil vary wildly, as do opinions on how they interact. Still, belief in some difference between that which is "good" and that which is "evil" pervades all of mankind. When all options and ideas are compared, only the Bible provides a perspective on good and evil that is fully coherent and fully livable (Got Questions, 2013).

Psalm 25:6-15 - "Remember, Lord, your great mercy and love, for they are from of old. Do not remember the sins of my youth and my rebellious ways; according to your love remember me, for you, Lord, are good. Good and upright is the Lord; therefore he instructs sinners in his ways. He guides the humble in what is right and teaches them his way. All the ways of the Lord are loving and faithful toward those who keep the demands of his covenant. For the sake of your name, Lord, forgive my iniquity, though it is great. Who, then, are those who fear the Lord? He will instruct them in the ways they should choose. They will spend their days in prosperity, and their descendants will inherit the land. The Lord confides in those who fear him; he makes his covenant known to them.

My eyes are ever on the LORD, for only he will release my feet from the snare" (**NIV**).

According to the Bible, "good versus evil" is not a matter of opinion. Nor is it an evenly matched struggle between two beings or forces. Scripture does not indicate that the boundaries of good and evil change. Nor does it claim the conflict between them will last forever. Of special importance is that the Bible does not suggest some people are good, while other people are evil. Rather, the Bible teaches that good and evil are defined in reference to a perfect and unchanging God. Every person must grapple individually with the presence and temptations of evil. Scripture notes that all evil, without exception, will ultimately be punished and defeated. And it tells us there is an ultimate standard of goodness to which we should aspire, a standard grounded in a person, rather than a theory (Got Questions, 2013).

- **Good and Evil Are Objectively Distinct**

According to the Bible, there is a real difference between good and evil. Some worldviews claim all moral distinctions are based purely on preference. Atheism, for instance, allows no objective basis for defining anything as "good" or "evil." In a godless universe, there are only things a person prefers and things a person does not prefer. This is a key reason why philosophies embracing atheism always tend toward violence and tyranny: there is no sense of higher authority and no reason to moderate the whims of those in power.

The idea that defining good and evil depends on preferences or situations is commonly called moral relativism. Scripture rejects this idea as false. The Bible defines some things as "good" and other things as "evil":

Isaiah 5:20 - "Woe to those who call evil good and good evil, who put darkness for light and light for darkness, who put bitter for sweet and sweet for bitter" (**NIV**).

Romans 12:9 - "Love must be sincere. Hate what is evil; cling to what is good" (**NIV**).

This dichotomy is reflected in the consistent use of themes such as light versus darkness:

Isaiah 9:2 - "The people walking in darkness have seen a great light; on those living in the land of deep darkness a light has dawned" (**NIV**).

Matthew 4:16 - "The people living in darkness have seen a great light; on those living in the land of the shadow of death a light has dawned" (**NIV**).

John 1:5 - "The light shines in the darkness, and the darkness has not overcome it" (**NIV**).

Ephesians 5:8 - "For you were once darkness, but now you are light in the Lord. Live as children of light" (**NIV**).

The ultimate fate of all people depends on whether they are aligned with a good God or opposed to Him.

I Corinthians 6:9-11 - "Or do you not know that wrongdoers will not inherit the kingdom of God? Do not be deceived: Neither the sexually immoral nor idolaters nor adulterers nor men who have sex with men nor thieves nor the greedy nor drunkards nor slanderers nor swindlers will inherit the kingdom of God. And that is what some of you were. But you were washed, you were sanctified, you were justified in the name of the Lord Jesus Christ and by the Spirit of our God" (**NIV**).

Revelation 21:8 - "But the cowardly, the unbelieving, the vile, the murderers, the sexually immoral, those who practice magic arts, the idolaters and all liars, they will be consigned to the fiery lake of burning sulfur. This is the second death" (**NIV**).

Discerning between good and evil is possible only in reference to a single, unchanging standard: the perfect nature of God. God is not subject to morality, since He is the source and benchmark for it. Nor is morality subject to change, since God's perfect nature is eternal and unchanging.

- **Good and Evil Are Not Balanced**

A frequent component of fiction and fantasy is the idea that good and evil are equally balanced, evenly matched forces. According to this view, neither is ultimately in control. Either may eventually win. This is the concept of dualism, which suggests a perpetual balance between the forces of good and evil. In some cases, dualism implies that opposing beings, such as God and Satan, are deadlocked in a struggle for control and power.

Some worldviews teach that all good and evil will eventually be balanced. This is related to Eastern ideas such as karma, which implies that good and evil are inherently imbalanced but will one day be evened out. Scripture rejects dualism as false. The Bible indicates that God is absolutely supreme and in no danger whatsoever of being defeated.

Job 42:2 - "I know that thou canst do all things, and that no purpose of thine can be thwarted" (**RSV**).

Psalm 89:8 - "O Lord God of hosts, who is mighty as thou art, O Lord, with thy faithfulness round about thee" (**RSV**)?

What Satan does, he is "allowed" to do, but he cannot act to overpower God.

Galations 6:7 - "Do not be deceived; God is not mocked, for whatever a man sows, that he will also reap" (**RSV**).

Job 1:12 - "And the Lord said to Satan, "Behold, all that he has is in your power; only upon himself do not put forth your hand." So Satan went forth from the presence of the Lord" (**RSV**).

Revelation 9:1 - "And the fifth angel blew his trumpet, and I saw a star fallen from heaven to earth, and he was given the key of the shaft of the bottomless pit" (**RSV**).

Revelation 20:7 - "And when the thousand years are ended, Satan will be loosed from his prison" (**RSV**).

Biblically, evil is destined only for defeat and destruction. Not one single act of evil will escape judgment; every sin will either be paid for in Christ on the cross,

II Corinthians 5:21 - "For our sake he made him to be sin who knew no sin, so that in him we might become the righteousness of God" (**RSV**).

Or by those who reject Christ:

John 3:36 - "He who believes in the Son has eternal life; he who does not obey the Son shall not see life, but the wrath of God rests upon him" (**RSV**).

As they experience an eternity in hell:

Revelation 21:11-15 - "Having the glory of God, its radiance like a most rare jewel, like a jasper, clear as crystal. It had a great, high wall, with twelve gates, and at the gates twelve angels, and on the gates the names of the twelve tribes of the sons of Israel were inscribed; on the east three gates, on the north three gates, on the south three gates, and on the west three gates. And the wall of the city had twelve foundations, and on them the twelve names of the twelve apostles of the Lamb. And he who talked to me had a measuring rod of gold to measure the city and its gates and walls" (**RSV**).

- **Good and Evil Are Not External**

Evidence that humanity holds to a basic concept of good versus evil is obvious.

Romans 1:18-20 - "For the wrath of God is revealed from heaven against all ungodliness and wickedness of men who by their wickedness suppress the truth. For what can be known about God is plain to them, because God has shown it to them. Ever since the creation of the world his invisible nature, namely, his eternal power and deity, has been clearly perceived in the things that have been made. So they are without excuse" (**RSV**).

This explains why moral reasoning, separating "what is" from "what ought to be", is a universal facet of humanity. Of course, that does not mean all people hold the same views on good and evil. We are not examining morality from the outside, as neutral observers; all moral discussions by definition involve the person(s) who discuss them, as well.

A unique aspect of the Bible's teaching on good and evil is that all people, without exception, are subject to sin and evil:

Romans 3:10 - "As it is written: There is no one righteous, not even one" (**NIV**).

Romans 3:23 - "For all have sinned and fall short of the glory of God" (**NIV**).

The biblical concept of a sin nature means that the line between good and evil cannot be drawn between people. Rather, it is drawn *within* every person. This fact of human nature is critical to understand.

Matthew 15:19-20 - "For out of the heart come evil thoughts, murder, adultery, sexual immorality, theft, false testimony, slander. These are what defile a person; but eating with unwashed hands does not defile them" (**NIV**).

As Aleksandr Solzhenitsyn famously said, "If only it were all so simple! If only there were evil people somewhere insidiously committing evil deeds, and it were necessary only to separate them from the rest of us and destroy them. But the line dividing good and evil cuts through the heart of every human being. And who is willing to destroy a piece of his own heart?" In simpler language, C.S. Lewis noted, "To be a Christian means to forgive the inexcusable because God has forgiven the inexcusable in you" (Solzhenitsyn, 2002).

Matthew 6:14-15 - "For if you forgive men their trespasses, your heavenly Father also will forgive you; but if you do not forgive men their trespasses, neither will your Father forgive your trespasses" (**RSV**).

The essential message of the gospel is that all people, without exception, are sinners in need of a Savior. Biblical Christianity does not see good versus evil as a battle to be fought on earth.

John 18:36 - "Jesus answered, "My kingship is not of this world; if my kingship were of this world, my servants would fight, that I might not be handed over to the Jews; but my kingship is not from the world" (**RSV**).

An issue to resolve by revenge or retribution:

Romans 12:20-21 - "No, "if your enemy is hungry, feed him; if he is thirsty, give him drink; for by so doing you will heap burning coals upon his head." Do not be overcome by evil, but overcome evil with good" (**RSV**).

Or a philosophical position to be considered. The Bible says every person is created for a good purpose.

Genesis 1:27 - "So God created man in his own image, in the image of God he created him; male and female he created them" (**RSV**).

Galatians 3:28 - "There is neither Jew nor Greek, there is neither slave nor free, there is neither male nor female; for you are all one in Christ Jesus" (**RSV**).

But suffers from an evil heart:

Romans 7:15-25 - "I do not understand my own actions. For I do not do what I want, but I do the very thing I hate. Now if I do what I do not want, I agree that the law is good. So then it is no longer I that do it, but sin which dwells within me. For I know that nothing good dwells within me, that is, in my flesh. I can will what is right, but I cannot do it. For I do not do the good I want, but the evil I do not want is what I do. Now if I do what I do not want, it is no longer I that do it, but sin which dwells within me. So I find it to be a law that when I want to do right, evil lies close at hand. For I delight in the law of God, in my inmost self, but I see in my members another law at war with the law of my mind and making me captive to the law of sin which dwells in my members. Wretched man that I am! Who will deliver me from this body of death? Thanks be to God through Jesus Christ our Lord! So then, I of myself serve the law of God with my mind, but with my flesh I serve the law of sin" (**RSV**).

Which can only be remedied by faith in Jesus Christ:

John 14:6 - Jesus said to him, "I am the way, and the truth, and the life; no one comes to the Father, but by me" (**RSV**).

Redemption is available to anyone:

Matthew 7:7-8 - "Ask, and it will be given you; seek, and you will find; knock, and it will be opened to you. For every one who asks receives, and he who seeks finds, and to him who knocks it will be opened" (**RSV**).

Revelation 22:15 - "Outside are the dogs and sorcerers and fornicators and murderers and idolaters, and every one who loves and practices falsehood" (**RSV**).

Regardless of his past or the depth of his sin:

I Corinthians 6:9-11 - "Do you not know that the unrighteous will not inherit the kingdom of God? Do not be deceived; neither the immoral, nor idolaters, nor adulterers, nor sexual perverts, nor thieves, nor the greedy, nor drunkards, nor revilers, nor robbers will inherit the kingdom of God. And such were some of you. But you were washed, you were sanctified, you were justified in the name of the Lord Jesus Christ and in the Spirit of our God" (**RSV**).

- **Good versus Evil Requires "Right Judgment"**

Another key aspect of the Bible's teaching on "good versus evil" is that no person is infallible, even on spiritual matters. Those who are guided by the Holy Spirit are better equipped to judge spiritual matters.

I Corinthians 2:14 - "The unspiritual man does not receive the gifts of the Spirit of God, for they are folly to him, and he is not able to understand them because they are spiritually discerned" (**RSV**).

And they ought to do so. Scripture is clear that all people are subject to sin, and it is just as clear that all people are subject to correction.

Hebrews 12:5-11 - "And have you forgotten the exhortation which addresses you as sons? "My son, do not regard lightly the discipline of the Lord, nor lose courage when you are punished by him. For the Lord disciplines him whom he loves, and chastises every son whom he receives." It is for discipline that you have to endure. God is treating you as sons; for what son is there whom his father does not discipline? If you are left without discipline, in which all have participated, then you are illegitimate children and not sons. Besides this, we have had earthly fathers to discipline us and we respected them. Shall we not much more be subject to the Father of spirits and live? For they disciplined us for a short time at their pleasure, but he disciplines us for our good, that we may share his holiness. For the moment all discipline seems painful rather than pleasant; later it yields the peaceful fruit of righteousness to those who have been trained by it" (**RSV**).

Learning:

II Timothy 2:15 - "Do your best to present yourself to God as one approved, a workman who has no need to be ashamed, rightly handling the word of truth" (**RSV**).

And limitations:

I Samuel 16:7 - "But the Lord said to Samuel, "Do not look on his appearance or on the height of his stature, because I have rejected him; for the Lord sees not as man sees; man looks on the outward appearance, but the Lord looks on the heart" (**RSV**).

In **Matthew 7**, Jesus gives an extensive explanation of how to properly discern between good and evil: to "judge" in the correct way; that is, to use "right judgment".

John 7:34 - "You will seek me and you will not find me; where I am you cannot come" (**RSV**).

The Bible commends examination:

Acts 17:11 - "Now these Jews were more noble than those in Thessalonica, for they received the word with all eagerness, examining the scriptures daily to see if these things were so" (**RSV**).

Commands putting things to the test:

I John 4:1 - "Beloved, do not believe every spirit, but test the spirits to see whether they are of God; for many false prophets have gone out into the world" (**RSV**).

And promotes accountability:

I Peter 3:15 - "But in your hearts reverence Christ as Lord. Always be prepared to make a defense to any one who calls you to account for the hope that is in you, yet do it with gentleness and reverence" (**RSV**).

And a commitment to truth:

Galatians 1:8-9 - "But even if we, or an angel from heaven, should preach to you a gospel contrary to that which we preached to you, let him be accursed. As we have said before, so now I say again, If any one is preaching to you a gospel contrary to that which you received, let him be accursed" (**RSV**).

Scripture does not imply that "good versus evil" is a simplistic, binary concept. Since only God is ultimately perfect, the Bible allows for a "good versus better" spectrum. God called His initial creation "good".

Genesis 1:24 - "Then God said, "Let the earth bring forth living creatures after their kind: cattle and creeping things and beasts of the earth after their kind"; and it was so" (**NASB**).

Then after more creating, He called it "very good".

Genesis 1:28 - "God blessed them; and God said to them, "Be fruitful and multiply, and fill the earth, and subdue it; and rule over the fish of the sea and over the birds of the sky and over every living thing that moves on the earth" (**NASB**).

Some of the good things God has given us have more than one use, and not all uses are automatically good or evil.

I Timothy 4:4 - "For everything created by God is good, and nothing is to be rejected if it is received with gratitude" (**NASB**).

The biblical understanding of good versus evil does not imply that all things are either perfectly holy or wholly satanic. Rather, there can be good and bad aspects of many of the freedoms God gives us.

I Corinthians 6:12 - "All things are lawful for me, but not all things are profitable. All things are lawful for me, but I will not be mastered by anything" (**NASB**).

Likewise, while all sin leads to separation from God, Scripture does speak of some sins as being more heinous than others. The Bible acknowledges that not every moment in human experience will come with a clear, black-and-white moral answer. Scripture focuses only on the most important points we need to know, not every imaginable scenario:

John 21:25 - "And there are also many other things which Jesus did, which if they were written in detail, I suppose that even the world itself would not contain the books that would be written" (**NASB**).

This means even the most sincere, Bible-believing, born-again Christians might disagree on an ethical question.

I Corinthians 10:23-33 - "All things are lawful, but not all things are profitable. All things are lawful, but not all things edify. Let no one seek his own *good*, but that of his [a]neighbor. Eat anything that is sold in the meat market without asking questions for conscience' sake; FOR THE EARTH IS THE LORD'S, AND ALL IT CONTAINS. If one of the unbelievers invites you and you want to go, eat anything that is set before you without asking questions for conscience' sake. But if anyone says to you, "This is meat sacrificed to idols," do not eat *it*, for the sake of the one who informed *you*, and for conscience' sake; I mean not your own conscience, but the other *man's*; for why is my freedom judged by another's conscience? If I partake with thankfulness, why am I slandered concerning that for which I give thanks? Whether, then, you eat or drink or whatever you do, do all to the glory of God. Give no offense either to Jews or to Greeks or to the church of God; just as I also please all men in all things, not seeking my own profit but the *profit* of the many, so that they may be saved" (**NASB**).

The Bible's answer, when the issue is not covered overtly in God's Word:

I Corinthians 5:6 - "Your boasting is not good. Do you not know that a little leaven leavens the whole lump *of dough*" (**NASB**)?

Is for tolerance and patience:

Titus 3:9 - "But avoid foolish controversies and genealogies and strife and disputes about the Law, for they are unprofitable and worthless" (**NASB**).

We're given a conscience for a reason:

Romans 14:23 - "But he who doubts is condemned if he eats, because *his eating is* not from faith; and whatever is not from faith is sin" (**NASB**).

Truth is objective; for any given opinion or interpretation, someone is right, and someone is wrong. But human beings lack the moral perfection of God; this is reflected in the Bible's teaching on good versus evil and our role in applying good judgment. Scripture encourages believers not to apply terms like *good, evil, sin,* and so forth to issues where there is room for doubt.

Romans 14:1-12 - "Now accept the one who is weak in faith, *but* not for *the purpose of* passing judgment on his opinions. One person has faith that he may eat all things, but he who is weak eats vegetables *only*. The one who eats is not to regard with contempt the one who does not eat, and the one who does not eat is not to judge the one who eats, for God has accepted him. Who are you to judge the [a]servant of another? To his own master he stands or falls; and he will stand, for the Lord is able to make him stand. One person regards one day above another, another regards every day *alike*. Each person must be fully convinced in his own mind. He who observes the day, observes it for the Lord, and he who eats, does so for the Lord, for he gives thanks to God; and he who eats not, for the

Lord he does not eat, and gives thanks to God. For not one of us lives for himself, and not one dies for himself; for if we live, we live for the Lord, or if we die, we die for the Lord; therefore whether we live or die, we are the Lord's. For to this end Christ died and lived again, that He might be Lord both of the dead and of the living. But you, why do you judge your brother? Or you again, why do you regard your brother with contempt? For we will all stand before the judgment seat of God. For it is written, "As I LIVE, SAYS THE LORD, EVERY KNEE SHALL BOW TO ME, AND EVERY TONGUE SHALL GIVE PRAISE TO GOD." So then each one of us will give an account of himself to God" (**NASB**).

Contrary to what some think, the Bible admits that human beings might not always be correct in our moral judgments. We are not to avoid all judgment:

John 7:24 - "Do not judge according to appearance, but judge with righteous judgment" (**NASB**).

But the Bible teaches us to carefully consider when and how we judge.

Ephesians 5:10 - "Trying to learn what is pleasing to the Lord" (**NASB**).

- **Good versus Evil Demands a Response**

The Bible's teaching on good versus evil leads to a challenging conclusion: that every person is obligated to make a fundamental choice between the two. That choice is entirely determined by our response to God, who is both the definition of good and our Creator. Moment by moment, that means either following His will or rebelling and choosing to sin.

I Corinthians 10:13 - "No temptation has overtaken you but such as is common to man; and God is faithful, who will not allow you to be tempted beyond what you are able, but with the temptation will provide the way of escape also, so that you will be able to endure it" (**NASB**).

Eternally, this means we either choose to accept Him and His salvation:

John 3:16 - "For God so loved the world, that He gave His only begotten Son, that whoever believes in Him shall not perish, but have eternal life" (**NASB**).

John 14:6 - "Jesus said to him, "I am the way, and the truth, and the life; no one comes to the Father but through Me" (**NASB**).

Or align ourselves against Him:

John 3:36 - "He who believes in the Son has eternal life; but he who does not obey the Son will not see life, but the wrath of God abides on him" (**NASB**).

While we may be imperfect and fallible, we cannot be neutral in our approach to good versus evil. Our hearts are either seeking the goodness of God:

Matthew 7:7-8 - "Ask, and it will be given to you; seek, and you will find; knock, and it will be opened to you. For everyone who asks receives, and he who seeks finds, and to him who knocks it will be opened" (**NASB**).

Romans 2:4 - "Or do you think lightly of the riches of His kindness and tolerance and patience, not knowing that the kindness of God leads you to repentance" (**NASB**)?

Redemption is available to anyone.

CHAPTER 15

HOW CAN I OVERCOME EVIL WITH GOOD?

These are difficult days in our country; 16 years from the attacks on the Twin Towers, the threat of terrorist violence still hangs over us and over freedom-loving people around the world. After many years of hoping for progress, anger and violence over issues of race have reached new intensity. Loss of civility and manners in public life is producing a new meanness of spirit that often makes life increasingly unmanageable in the classroom, work place, and all too often in the home (GQM, 2019).

On top of all this, the shared sense of right and wrong that has bound our people together in this country for centuries has in large measure been discarded and swept away. Our nation is deeply divided over issues of life, marriage, gender, and even death. Having lost the sense of living under the authority of God, our culture increasingly feels the liberty to take great issues into our hands and do with them as we please. All over our country, believing people are asking, "What in the world are we to do?" The answer to that question is found in **Romans 12**.

Romans 12:9-20 - "9 Love must be sincere. Hate what is evil; cling to what is good. 10 Be devoted to one another in love. Honor one another above yourselves. 11 Never be lacking in zeal, but keep your spiritual fervor, serving the Lord. 12 Be joyful in hope, patient in affliction, faithful in prayer. 13 Share with the Lord's people who are in need. Practice hospitality. 14 Bless those who persecute you; bless and do not curse. 15 Rejoice with those who rejoice; mourn with those who mourn. 16 Live in harmony with one another. Do not be proud, but be willing to associate with people of low position. Do not be conceited. 17 Do not repay anyone evil for evil. Be careful to do what is right in the eyes of everyone. 18 If it is possible, as far as it depends on you, live at peace with everyone. 19 Do not take revenge, my dear friends, but leave room for God's wrath, for it is written: "It is mine to avenge; I will repay," says the Lord. 20 On the contrary: "If your enemy is hungry, feed him; if he is thirsty, give him something to drink. In doing this, you will heap burning coals on his head." 21 Do not be overcome by evil, but overcome evil with good" (**NIV**).

This verse follows exhortations such as "Bless those who persecute you" (verse 14) and "Do not repay anyone evil for evil" (verse 17). The theme of the passage is how to love with sincerity (verse 9), and the instructions require us to set aside our natural inclinations. God's way always challenges our fleshly nature and calls us to live at a higher level by the Spirit's power. The human way is to curse those who curse us and try to overcome evil with more evil. But, according to:

Romans 12:21 - "Do not be overcome by evil, but overcome evil with good" (**NIV**).

We can overcome evil with good because God's Goodness is stronger than any evil.

Jesus was the perfect example of overcoming evil with good:

I Peter 2:23 - "When they hurled their insults at him, he did not retaliate; when he suffered, he made no threats. Instead, he entrusted himself to him who judges justly" (**NIV**).

In submitting Himself to the evil of His captors, He conquered sin, Satan, and death.

Ephesians 4:8-10 - "This is why it says: "When he ascended on high, he took many captives and gave gifts to his people." (What does "he ascended" mean except that he also descended to the lower, earthly regions? He who descended is the very one who ascended higher than all the heavens, in order to fill the whole universe.)" (**NIV**).

Evil thought it won that day when it nailed Christ to the cross. But because Jesus was fully surrendered to the will and plan of His Father, the Son of God overcame their evil with good. Though the actions against Christ were in themselves evil, Jesus' death and later resurrection overcame that evil by purchasing forgiveness and eternal life for everyone who would believe:

John 1:12 - "Yet to all who did receive him, to those who believed in his name, he gave the right to become children of God" (**NIV**).

John 3:16-18 - "For God so loved the world that he gave his one and only Son, that whoever believes in him shall not perish but have eternal life. For God did not send his Son into the world to condemn the world, but to save the world through him. Whoever believes in him is not condemned, but whoever does not believe stands condemned already because they have not believed in the name of God's one and only Son" (**NIV**).

John 20:31 - "But these are written that you may believe that Jesus is the Messiah, the Son of God, and that by believing you may have life in his name" (**NIV**).

We overcome evil the same way, with good. The Lord says that vengeance belongs to Him and He will repay:

Hebrews 10:30 - "For we know him who said, "It is mine to avenge; I will repay," and again, "The Lord will judge his people" (**NIV**).

We can entrust ourselves to God, just like Jesus did, and know that He will work even those evil acts committed against us for our good.

Genesis 50:20 - "You intended to harm me, but God intended it for good to accomplish what is now being done, the saving of many lives" (**NIV**).

Romans 8:28 - "And we know that in all things God works for the good of those who love him, who have been called according to his purpose" (**NIV**).

When we refuse to respond in kind to those who would persecute us, their evil actions stand alone, whereas retaliation brings us down to the level of the instigators. When two people are fighting, and one is clearly attacking the other, evil is highlighted for all to see. When we return a soft word, a kindness, or generosity to someone who has wronged us, we leave the perpetrator alone in his evil.

Proverbs 25:21-22 says, "If your enemy is hungry, give him food to eat; if he is thirsty, give him water to drink. In doing this, you will heap burning coals on his head, and the Lord will reward you" (**NIV**).

Paul quotes this passage in:

Romans 12:20 - "But if your enemy is hungry, feed him, and if he is thirsty, give him a drink; for in so doing you will heap burning coals on his head" (**NASB**).

Just before his command to "overcome evil with good." To "heap burning coals on his head" probably refers to the natural response of the enemy to kindness. Nothing makes us feel more shamed and embarrassed by our actions than someone reacting to our hurtful behavior with gentle forgiveness. Kindness in the face of unkindness demonstrates the stark contrast between the two. The goal of a gentle reaction to the enemy is not to embarrass or get the last word but to help facilitate repentance in the evildoer (GQM, 2019).

If we remember a few key things, we are on our way to overcoming evil with good. I am not the judge; God is.

He will do what is right

- **Genesis 18:25** - "Far be it from You to do such a thing, to slay the righteous with the wicked, so that the righteous and the wicked are treated alike. Far be it from You! Shall not the Judge of all the earth deal justly" (**NASB**)?

As a Christian, my response to evil should not copy the world's behavior but reflect Christ, who is in me.

- **Romans 12:1-2** - "Therefore I urge you, brethren, by the mercies of God, to present your bodies a living and holy sacrifice, acceptable to God, *which is* your spiritual service of worship. And do not be conformed to this world, but be transformed by the renewing of your mind, so that you may prove what the will of God is, that which is good and [e]acceptable and perfect" (**NASB**).

Keeping my eyes on Jesus helps me know how to respond when I am treated poorly.

- **Romans 12:2** - "And do not be conformed to this world, but be transformed by the renewing of your mind, so that you may prove what the will of God is, that which is good and acceptable and perfect" (**NASB**).

Jesus reminded the Pharisees that Satan cannot drive out Satan.

- **Matthew 12:25-28** - "And knowing their thoughts Jesus said to them, "Any kingdom divided against itself is laid waste; and any city or house divided against itself will not stand. If Satan casts out Satan, he is divided against himself; how then will his kingdom stand? If I by Beelzebul cast out demons, by whom do your sons cast *them* out? For this reason they will be your judges. But if I cast out demons by the Spirit of God, then the kingdom of God has come upon you" (**NASB**).

Likewise, evil cannot drive out evil. An evil response only doubles the evil. When we respond to evil in humility and grace, we are proving that good triumphs over wickedness. We cannot stop people from doing evil, but they cannot force us to participate with them. It takes no power, might, or wisdom to retaliate against evildoers. But returning good for evil is one of the greatest demonstrations of strength.

We can entrust ourselves to God!

REFERENCES

Forrester, Christina, *Calling Good What Is Evil And Evil What Is Good*, HuffPost, February 16, 2016.

Got Questions Ministries, *What does the Bible say about good versus evil?*, May 13, 2019.

Got Questions Ministries, *What is the definition of evil?*, February 14, 2012.

Graham, Billy, *Calling Evil Good*, Decision Magazine, Billy Graham Evangelistic Association, February 12, 2012

Graham, Billy, *Confusing Evil With Good*, Decision Magazine, October 01, 2018.

Hattangadi, Vidya, *Can ethics be taught*, Higher Education Journal, May 21, 2014.

Hulme, David, *Right and Wrong*, Ethics and Morality, Fall, 2000.

Jameson, Jeremiah, End Times Prophecy Report, May 14, 2016.

Markham, Laura, *How Do Children Learn Right from Wrong?*, Psychology Today, Sussex Publishers, LLC, March 7, 2017.

Romig, Rollo, *What Do We Mean By "Evil"?*, The New Yorker, July 25, 2012

Smith, Colin, *How to Overcome Evil with Good*, Crosswalk September 11, 2017.

Snoke, David, *Natural vs. moral evil*, Christian Scientific Society, January 24, 2016.

Solzhenitsyn, Aleksandr, The Gulag Archipelago, Harper Collins, 2002.

Taylor, Steve, The Real Meaning of 'Good' and 'Evil', Sussex Publishers, August 26, 2013.

The Holy Bible, *King James Version,* (KJV), New York: American Bible Society, 1999.

The Holy Bible, *New American Standard Bible,* (NASB), La Habra, CA: Foundation Publications, for the Lockman Foundation, 1971.

The Holy Bible, *New International Version,* (NIV), Grand Rapids: Zondervan Publishing House, 1984.

The Holy Bible, *New Living Translation,* (NLT), Tyndale House Foundation, 2015.

The Holy Bible, *New Revised Standard Version Bible,* (RSV), Division of Christian Education of the National Council of the Churches of Christ in the United States of America, 1989.

Weinstein, Edie, *Right, Wrong or Indifferent: Finding a Moral Compass,* Psych Central, October 8, 2018.

Wellman, Jack, *Right Vs. Wrong: How to Answer This from the Bible,* August 4, 2012.

APPENDIX

SCRIPTURES ON GOOD AND EVIL

James 4:17   Therefore to him that knoweth to do good, and doeth not, to him it is sin.

Isaiah 5:20   Woe unto them that call evil good, and good evil; that put darkness for light, and light for darkness; that put bitter for sweet, and sweet for bitter!

John 3:19-21   And this is the condemnation, that light is come into the world, and men loved darkness rather than light, because their deeds were evil.

Romans 13:1   Let every soul be subject unto the higher powers. For there is no power but of God: the powers that be are ordained of God.

Romans 7:15-22   For that which I do I allow not: for what I would, that do I not; but what I hate, that do I.

Mark 7:20   And he said, That which cometh out of the man, that defileth the man.

Romans 13:8-10	Owe no man any thing, but to love one another: for he that loveth another hath fulfilled the law.
Proverbs 14:12	There is a way which seemeth right unto a man, but the end thereof the ways of death.
Proverbs 22:6	Train up a child in the way he should go: and when he is old, he will not depart from it.
Matthew 28:18	And Jesus came and spake unto them, saying, All power is given unto me in heaven and in earth.
Colossians 3:17	And whatsoever ye do in word or deed, [do] all in the name of the Lord Jesus, giving thanks to God and the Father by him.
I Timothy 6:10	For the love of money is the root of all evil: which while some coveted after, they have erred from the faith, and pierced themselves through with many sorrows.
Ephesians 6:4	And, ye fathers, provoke not your children to wrath: but bring them up in the nurture and admonition of the Lord.
Revelation 3:16	So then because thou art lukewarm, and neither cold nor hot, I will spue thee out of my mouth.
Ephesians 4:28	Let him that stole steal no more: but rather let him labour, working with His hands the thing which is good, that he may have to give to him that needeth.

I Timothy 4:12   Let no man despise thy youth; but be thou an example of the believers, in word, in conversation, in charity, in spirit, in faith, in purity.

Romans 1:21   Because that, when they knew God, they glorified [him] not as God, neither were thankful; but became vain in their imaginations, and their foolish heart was darkened.

Psalms 119:55   I have remembered thy name, O LORD, in the night, and have kept thy law.

Printed in the United States
By Bookmasters